# A Taste of Italy

# Traditional Italian Cooking Made Easy with Authentic Italian Recipes

## Sarah Spencer

This book is presented solely for motivational and informational purposes. The author and the publisher do not hold any responsibility for errors, omissions, or contrary interpretation of the subject matter herein. The recipes provided in this book are for informational purposes only and are not intended to provide dietary advice. A medical practitioner should be consulted before making any changes in diet. Additionally, recipes' cooking times may require adjustment depending on age and quality of appliances. Readers are strongly urged to take all precautions to ensure ingredients are fully cooked in order to avoid the dangers of foodborne illnesses.

*ISBN: 9781070137636*

*Printed in the United States*

— THE —
COOK BOOK
PUBLISHER
www.thecookbookpublisher.com

# CONTENTS

# COOKING ITALIAN

Italy's food culture revolves around recipes deeply rooted in the sea and earth, bringing together centuries-old traditions to produce simple, sun-soaked flavors. A plate full of classic Italian cuisine on a calm evening is an absolute pleasure. The meals are a family-focused and unfussy celebration of food. Whether cooked quickly or painstakingly prepared for hours, the meals made by Italian mothers and grandmothers are always simple, achievable and beautiful, featuring local, seasonal ingredients and providing authentic home vibes. Gastronomes from around the world love to savor the unique aromas and rich flavors of Italian regional cuisine, and the colorful dishes never fail to astonish with their visual appeal.

## Italian Ingredients

Italian cooking is loaded with simple yet exciting flavors. It is well-known for wholesome ingredients that make the meals tasty as well as healthy.

### Olive Oil
Olive oil is consumed in large quantities in Italy and is called "the golden liquid" in Italian cooking. The most popular Italian recipes are incomplete without olive oil. Loaded with monounsaturated fatty acids and noted for its anti-inflammatory properties, extra-virgin olive oil provides abundant health benefits and plays a vital part in many Mediterranean recipes.

### Cheese
The love for cheese in Italian cooking is incredible. Cheeses like pecorino, burrata, Parmesan, mascarpone, ricotta, and mozzarella make their appearance not only in internationally famous pizzas and pasta dishes but in everything from appetizers and salads to desserts, toasted breads and other baked recipes.

### Tomatoes
Tomato is another essential ingredient for Italian cooking. Every amazing spaghetti and pizza sauce has some tomato in it. Tomato is used in abundance during winter, but Italians make good use of all the different seasonal varieties.

## Basil

Basil is highly appreciated in Mediterranean cooking and is used in many soups and salads. Pesto sauce prepared from basil makes an ideal complement to fish and poultry meals, breads, pasta and potato dishes.

## Pasta

Pasta is the pride of Italian food culture. For Italians, pasta is not just about macaroni, spaghetti, or even tagliatelle. Italians eat multiple kinds of short pasta, long pasta, baked pasta, stuffed pasta and so on. Popular pasta varieties include fusilli, ravioli, macaroni, spaghetti, fettuccine, penne, pappardelle, and tagliatelle.

## Meat & Prosciutto

Usually accompanied by legumes and fresh vegetables, Italian meat courses may be poultry, pork, lamb, or beef. Dry cured ham products from Italy are popular in many countries. Prosciutto is used in many pasta dishes, pizzas, and other main course meals.

## Oregano & Rosemary

Rosemary is treated like the queen of herbs in Italian cuisine. Its delightful aroma features most commonly in risotto, pasta, and salads. A sprinkle of dried oregano adds flavor to many pizza, salad, and pasta recipes. It is also used to give an aromatic touch in many sauces.

## Garlic

Known for its medicinal properties, garlic shines as the star that makes Italian cooking more aromatic and healthier. Jarred garlic is avoided and fresh garlic is preferred to add more flavor.

## Porcini Mushrooms

Mushrooms are often referred to as "piglets" in Italian. Italian vegetarian recipes use mushrooms in abundance to provide a meat-like texture and enhance the flavor profile. They are also used in vegetarian and non-vegetarian risotto, soup, stew and polenta recipes.

## Wine

Wine is used in many sauces and as a cooking liquid to prepare main course meals including pasta and risotto. The alcohol in wine evaporates during cooking, leaving behind only the lovely flavors.

Other commonly used ingredients include capers, vinegar, beans, rice, potatoes, flour, legumes, broccoli, zucchini, and eggplant.

# Italian Meals

Lunch in Italy is usually served after antipasto, a common appetizer that Italians enjoy before having their main meal. Antipasto can be hot or cold. Then comes the *primo piatto* (first course). Soup, salad, and risotto are common choices for the *primo piatto*. After that may come the *secondi piatto* (second course), although not all Italians like to eat two courses for lunch. If served, the *secondi piatto* usually includes a meat or seafood dish with an optional side dish such as baked vegetables or a salad.

Dinner for Italians is an opportunity to spend quality time with their family and friends. Dinner is usually taken together with all family members to end the day on a good note. Just like lunch, it starts with an appetizer followed by one or two meal courses, which may be pasta and pizza as well as meat or seafood dishes. Pizza is usually cooked in a brick oven. Dessert is always served after dinner; however, some people also have dessert after lunch.

# The Recipes

This book presents some of the best classic recipes from Italian kitchens. Explore a special collection of much loved and much appreciated Italian recipes such as Tomato Alla Griglia, Alla Genovese Pesto, Parmesan Stuffed Mushrooms, Tangy Cicerchia Soup, Cauliflower Olive Salad, Pomodoro Basil Spaghetti, Pancetta Bucatini, Fagioli Bean Pasta, Veneto Peas Risotto, Chicken Polo Marsala, Chicken Polo Marsala, and many more. This book covers a diverse range of Italian dishes (appetizers, sides, pasta, pizza, risotto, poultry mains, meat mains, vegetarian dishes, and desserts) to cater to all your cooking needs.

Now get ready to cook classic Italian recipes in true Italian style!

# APPETIZERS

## Baked Sausage Zucchini

*Serves 4 | Prep. time 15 minutes | Cooking time 25 minutes*

### Ingredients

3 pork sausages, casings removed
4 medium zucchini, cut lengthwise
½ cup bread crumbs
½ cup mozzarella, shredded
½ cup Parmesan or Grana Padano cheese, grated
3 tablespoons olive oil
Nonstick cooking spray as needed
Salt and pepper to taste
Tomato sauce for serving

### Directions

1. Preheat the oven to 400°F. Grease a baking dish evenly with cooking spray.
2. Remove some of the flesh from inside the zucchini halves.
3. Finely chop the flesh and add it to a mixing bowl.
4. Add the sausage, bread crumbs, salt, mozzarella, Parmesan and oil. Combine well. Season with salt and pepper to taste.
5. Add the mixture into the zucchini halves. Arrange them on the prepared baking dish. Sprinkle some more grated cheese and drizzle olive oil on top.
6. Bake for 25 minutes. Serve warm with tomato sauce drizzled on top.

# Classic Basil Pesto

*Yields about 1 ¼ cups | Prep. time 20 minutes | Cooking time 0 minutes*

## *Ingredients*
2 tablespoons pine nuts
2 cloves garlic, or more to taste
1 bunch basil leaves
½ cup extra-virgin olive oil
½ cup Parmigiano-Reggiano cheese, grated
1½ tablespoons pecorino romano cheese, grated
Hot cooked pasta for serving

### Directions

1. Crush the garlic cloves with a mortar and pestle. Add the pine nuts and continue crushing.
2. Mix in the basil leaves, olive oil, and crush to make a smooth paste.
3. Mix in the cheeses and combine using a spoon.
4. Blend well and serve over cooked pasta.

Note: using a motor is the traditional way to make the pesto but you can also use a blender or a food processor and blend until you obtain the desired consistency. Olive oil should be added last very slowly to let the pesto emulsified.

# Padano Bean Spread

*Yields about 1½ cups | Prep. time 8–10 minutes | Cooking time 0 minutes*

## Ingredients

2 (15-ounce) cans cannellini beans, rinsed and drained

Juice and zest of 1 lemon

2 cloves garlic

3–4 tablespoons extra-virgin olive oil

3–4 tablespoons Grana Padano cheese, grated

Ground black pepper and salt to taste

A few sprigs Italian flat-leaf parsley

## Directions

1. In a blender, combine the cannellini beans, garlic, lemon juice, and zest and parsley; blend until pureed.
2. Slowly add in the oil while blending until well combined.
3. Add the mixture to a bowl and mix in the grated cheese. Season with salt and pepper to taste.
4. Transfer to a serving dish. Serve with Italian bread or vegetables.

# Parmesan Stuffed Mushrooms

*Serves 4 | Prep. time 8–10 minutes | Cooking time 20 minutes*

## Ingredients

12 large white mushrooms, cleaned and stemmed
2 cloves garlic, finely chopped
2 tablespoons parsley, chopped
¼ cup olive oil
½ cup Parmesan cheese, grated, plus extra
¾ cup bread crumbs, plus extra
Salt to taste
Nonstick cooking spray as needed

## Directions

1. Preheat the oven to 400°F. Grease a baking sheet evenly with cooking spray.
2. Finely chop the mushroom stems and add them to a mixing bowl.
3. Add the oil, bread crumbs, garlic, parsley, Parmesan cheese, and salt. Combine well.
4. Add some salt to the inside part of the mushroom caps and stuff them with the mixture.
5. Place them on the baking sheet and sprinkle with a pinch of bread crumbs and Parmesan cheese.
6. Bake for 20 minutes and serve warm.

# Tomato Alla Griglia

*Serves 6 | Prep. time 10 minutes | Cooking time 5 minutes*

## Ingredients

6–7 small tomatoes
1 cup breadcrumbs
⅛ teaspoon oregano
¼ cup Parmesan cheese, grated
1 tablespoon butter, melted
1 clove garlic, finely chopped
Salt and ground black pepper to taste
Oregano to taste

### Directions

1. Combine the breadcrumbs and ⅛ teaspoon oregano.
2. Cut the tomatoes into halves crosswise. Sprinkle them with chopped garlic, salt, and pepper.
3. Top with the breadcrumb mixture, butter, and cheese.
4. Place in a baking dish and broil for 5 minutes or until bubbly and tender.
5. Serve warm.

# Fried Zucchinis

*Serves 6 | Prep. time 20 minutes | Cooking time 20 minutes*

### Ingredients

3 zucchinis, sliced
1 cup bread crumbs
¼ cup Parmesan cheese, grated
2 teaspoons garlic powder
½ teaspoon freshly ground black pepper
1 teaspoon dried parsley
½ teaspoon dried oregano
2 eggs, beaten
Olive oil (about 1 cup)

Salt
Paprika

## Directions
1. Mix together breadcrumbs, Parmesan, garlic powder, pepper, parsley, and oregano, and place in a shallow dish.
2. Dip zucchini slices into beaten eggs then into bread crumbs. Press gently, and roll to cover all sides. Place zucchini slices on a clean plate in a single layer.
3. Heat olive oil in a large skillet to medium-high heat. When the oil is very hot, fry each zucchini until golden crisp, about 3–4 minutes, turning halfway through cooking. Drain on paper towels.
4. Sprinkle zucchini with paprika, and serve with tomato sauce for dipping.

# Eggplant Parmesan Appetizers

*Serves 4 | Prep. time 25 minutes | Cooking time 40 minutes*

**Ingredients**

1 large eggplant, peeled and sliced ¼-inch thick

⅓ cup milk

⅓ cup Italian seasoned breadcrumbs

½ cup olive oil

1 ½ cups tomato sauce

⅓ cup Parmesan cheese, grated plus some more for topping

Basil leaves

## *Directions*

1. Preheat oven to 400°F.
2. Salt the eggplant slices on both sides. Let rest for 15-20 minutes to get rid of excess moisture trapped in the eggplant. Place in a strainer. With paper towels carefully wipe the salt and water off the eggplant slices on both sides.
3. Dip sliced eggplant into milk, then coat with breadcrumbs on both sides. Place in a single layer on a dish until all have been coated. Heat olive oil in a skillet to medium-high heat. When the oil is very hot, reduce heat to medium. Cook each slice about 2 minutes on each side or until golden brown.
4. In a baking dish, spoon tomato sauce onto each eggplant, and top with Parmesan cheese. Heat in oven about 10 to 12 minutes until bubbly.
5. To serve, garnish with basil leaves, and sprinkle with Parmesan

# Bruschetta

*Serves 8 | Prep. time: 25 minutes | Cooking time 3-5 minutes*

## Ingredients

8 ripe Italian tomatoes (plum)
2 garlic cloves, crushed
2 tablespoons extra-virgin olive oil
2 teaspoons balsamic vinegar
1 teaspoon Italian spices
1 bunch basil leaves, chopped
Salt and freshly ground pepper to season
1 loaf of Italian bread
¼ cup extra-virgin olive oil

## Directions

1. Preheat the oven to 450ºF
2. Skin the tomatoes (cut an x in the skins and place into just-boiled water; turn off heat and leave for 1 minute). You should now be able to peel off the skin.

19

3. Cut tomatoes into halves, and then quarters, and remove the seeds and juice. Plum tomatoes are best for this recipe as they have fewer seeds and less juice than most.
4. Chop the tomatoes finely. Add to a bowl with olive oil, balsamic vinegar, garlic. Mix and season to taste.
5. Slice the bread/baguette diagonally so you have ½-inch slices. Use the ¼ cup of oil to coat one side of the bread. Place on a baking sheet, oil side down.
6. Toast each side of bread until golden brown, about a minute per side. Take a knife and score each side a few times. Rub some garlic into the slices and pour a ½ teaspoon of olive oil on each side.
7. Top with the tomato mix, garnish each toast with a fresh basil leave. Serve immediately so the bread does not get soggy.

# Tuscan White Bean Spread

*Yields about 2 cups | Prep. time: 15 minutes | Cooking time 0*

## Ingredients

¼ cup pancetta (Italian bacon), cooked crisp and chopped
1 15-oz. can cannellini beans
3 cloves garlic, minced
¼ cup onion, minced
3 tablespoons extra-virgin olive oil, divided
½ teaspoon salt
Fresh ground black pepper
Pasley for garnish

## Directions

1. Cook bacon or pancetta in 1 tablespoon of the olive oil until crisp. Set aside.

2. Combine beans, garlic, onion, 1 tablespoon olive oil, salt, and pepper in a food processor. Pulse until smooth. Transfer to serving dish.
3. Stir in bacon or pancetta until blended. Top with final 1 tablespoon olive oil drizzled on top. Can be chilled until serving.
4. Serve with fresh baguette slices or raw vegetables.

# Mozzarella Sticks

*Serves 12 | Prep. time 10 minutes | Cooking time 5 minutes*

**Ingredients**

1 cup Italian style bread crumbs
2 eggs
1 tablespoon milk
1 pound mozzarella cheese, cut into ¾-inch x ¾-inch strips
1 cup vegetable oil
Tomato sauce for dipping
Fresh basil for garnish

### *Directions*

1. In a bowl, whisk the eggs and milk together.
2. Place the bread crumbs in another bowl, or on a tray.
3. Dip the cheese in the egg mixture first, then the bread crumbs.
4. Dip it in the egg mixture and then the bread crumbs a second time, making sure to coat the cheese evenly.
5. Heat the oil in skillet.
6. Fry the cheese until golden brown, about 1 minute on each side. Do not fry too long, or the cheese will leak.
7. Drain on paper towels.
8. Serve with tomato sauce and sprinkle with finely chopped basil.

# Arancini Deep-Fried Rice Balls

*Serves 6 | Prep. time 15 minutes | Cooking time 15 minutes*

## Ingredients
1 cup Italian style seasoned bread crumbs

For filling
2 cups cooked arborio rice, cooled
½ cup Italian style seasoned bread crumbs
½ cup Parmesan, finely grated
¼ cup fresh basil leaves, finely chopped
2 eggs, beaten
4 ounces Gorgonzola, cut into ½-inch cubes
Vegetable oil, for frying

## *Directions*

1. Put the bread crumbs in a medium bowl, and set them aside.
2. Combine the rice, bread crumbs, Parmesan, basil, and eggs.
3. Scoop out about 2 tablespoons of the rice mixture at a time, and shape it into 1 ¾-inch balls. Dampen your hands so the rice doesn't stick them.
4. Insert a cube of Gorgonzola into each ball, and seal to cover the cheese.
5. Coat the balls with bread crumbs.
6. Fill a heavy-bottomed skillet or saucepan with oil to about 2-3 inches deep.
7. Heat over medium heat until a cube of bread will brown in about 2 minutes. Oil should be at 350°F.
8. Fry the balls, turning occasionally, until golden, about 4 to 5 minutes. Do not overcrowd the pan.
9. Drain on paper towels and serve.

# Asparagus Prosciutto

*Serves 4 | Prep. time 5 minutes | Cooking time 10–15 minutes*

## Ingredients
1 bunch asparagus
2 tablespoons olive oil
¼ pound prosciutto, cut in half lengthwise
2 tablespoons Parmesan cheese, grated
Nonstick cooking spray as needed

## Directions
1. Preheat the oven to 400°F / 204°C. Grease a baking dish evenly with cooking spray.
2. Trim the bottom 1½–2 inches of the asparagus stalks, keep the ends.
3. Arrange the asparagus spears on the baking dish. Add the cheese and oil and toss until well coated.
4. Wrap a half slice of the prosciutto around the lower half of each asparagus spear.
5. Arrange the spears prosciutto-seam-down in the baking dish. Bake for 10–12 minutes and serve warm.

# SOUPS AND SALADS

## Cicerchia Soup

*Serves 6 | Prep. time 10 minutes | Cooking time 15–20 minutes*

### Ingredients

3 tablespoons olive oil
½ small onion, chopped
1 quart vegetable broth
2 (15-ounce) cans chickpeas, drained and rinsed
¾ pound spinach, chopped
2 carrots, peeled and finely diced
1 (14-ounce) can diced tomatoes
Freshly ground black pepper and salt to taste

## Directions

1. Heat the oil in a large pot or saucepan over medium heat.
2. Add the onion and carrots; stir-cook to soften until translucent.
3. Add the tomatoes and broth; combine and bring to a boil.
4. Add the chickpeas and spinach; stir and simmer for 15 minutes.
5. Add salt and pepper to taste and top with additional olive oil if desired.
6. Serve warm.

# Tortellini Sausage Soup

*Serves 4 | Prep. time 10 minutes | Cooking time 60 minutes*

## Ingredients

1 pound Italian sausage
1 small onion, diced
2 cloves garlic, minced
½ cup white wine
½ cup water
3 cups chicken broth
1 (8-ounce) can tomato sauce
1 (16-ounce) can Italian stewed tomatoes, chopped (undrained)
1 cup carrots, sliced thin
1 teaspoon basil leaves, dried
2 tablespoons fresh parsley
½ teaspoon oregano

1 (½-pound) package tortellini
2 cup spinach
Shredded Parmesan cheese for serving

## Directions

1. Add the sausage to a medium saucepan or skillet over medium heat. Stir-cook to evenly brown.
2. Add the onion and garlic; stir-cook for 1 more minute.
3. Add the remaining Ingredients except for the zucchini and tortellini.
4. Simmer for 25–30 minutes.
5. Add the tortellini. Stir and simmer for an additional 25–30 minutes, until the pasta is cooked well.
6. About 5 minutes before the soup is ready, add the spinach. Continue cooking until the spinach are wilted.
7. Serve warm with shredded Parmesan cheese.

# Minestrone

*Serves 6 | Prep. time 10 minutes | Cooking time 35 minutes*

### Ingredients

2 tablespoons olive oil

1 medium potato, diced, about 1 cup

2 tablespoons onion, diced

1 carrot, cubed, about ½ cup

1 celery stalk, sliced

2 cloves garlic, peeled and sliced

1 cup zucchini, diced

2 (15-ounce) cans low-sodium chicken broth

1 (15-ounce)can cannelloni beans

1 (14-ounce) can Italian-style stewed tomatoes
Salt and freshly ground pepper
1 cup small pasta, uncooked
Parmesan cheese

## Directions

1. In a saucepan, heat olive oil over medium heat. Add potato, onion, and carrot. Cook 5–7 minutes until vegetables are softened, then add all remaining ingredients except pasta, and bring to a boil. Reduce heat, let simmer for 20-25 minutes.
2. Add pasta, and continue cooking until pasta is done, about 13-15 minutes. Season the minestrone with salt and pepper to taste.
3. To serve, ladle into soup bowls. Top with Parmesan cheese.

# Tortellini in Chicken Broth

*Serves 6 | Prep. time 15 minutes | Cooking time 60 minutes*

## Ingredients

3-4 pounds chicken parts on bone
2 cups fresh celery tops, chopped
12 cups water (or chicken stock)
2 teaspoons dried thyme
2 teaspoons dried sage
3 cloves garlic, minced
¾ cup carrot, sliced
¾ cup celery, diced
¼ cup green onions, diced

3 tablespoons fresh parsley, minced
Sea salt and freshly ground pepper
2 bay leaves
1 package cheese tortellini, about 2 cups

## *Directions*

1. Combine chicken, celery tops, thyme, and sage in 12 cups water in large stockpot. Bring to a boil, and reduce heat. Cover and simmer about 30 minutes until chicken is cooked.
2. Measure 6 cups of strained broth into another stock pot (store remaining chicken and broth). Add next 8 remaining ingredients. Cover and simmer over medium heat until vegetables are tender, about 15 minutes.
3. Add tortellini and cook per pasta directions, about 12-15 minutes. Remove bay leaves. Taste and adjust seasonings with salt and pepper.

# Pasta Fagioli Soup

*Serves 6 | Prep. time 5 minutes | Cooking time 30 minutes*

## *Ingredients*

1 tablespoon olive oil
1 pound ground beef
¼ cup diced pancetta (optional)
1 small onion, diced
2 small carrots, sliced
1 small red bell pepper, diced
1 (28-ounce) can diced tomatoes, undrained
1 (16-ounce) can white kidney beans, drained
2 cups beef stock
1 ½ teaspoons oregano
1 teaspoon pepper
3 teaspoons parsley
1 (10-ounce) jar tomato sauce
1 cup ditalini or pasta of choice, cooked according to packaging instructions
Grated Parmesan

## Directions

1. Heat the oil and brown the beef in a skillet.
2. Add the pancetta (optional) and sauté until lightly browned.
3. Add the onion, carrots, and pepper and sauté until tender (about 5 minutes).
4. Transfer the mixture to a soup pot, draining away the fat.
5. Add the rest of the ingredients EXCEPT the pasta and Parmesan, and bring them to a boil. Reduce the heat to simmer.
6. Simmer, stirring occasionally, until the vegetables are tender and the soup has the desired thickness (8-10 minutes).
7. Add the cooked ditalini, and cook to heat through (about 1 minute).
8. Serve sprinkled with grated Parmesan.

# Rice and Pesto Soup

*Serves 6 | Prep. time 10 minutes | Cooking time 45–50 minutes*

## Ingredients

2 cups green cabbage, finely shredded
2 cups Swiss chard, finely shredded
½ cup parsley, minced
7 cups chicken stock or water
⅓ cup uncooked Italian rice
1 cup basil pesto
Freshly ground pepper and salt to taste

## Directions

1. Add the stock/water, cabbage, greens and parsley to a large pot. Bring to a boil.
2. Reduce heat, cover and simmer for 20–30 minutes.
3. Stir in the rice; continue simmering, covered, for 8–10 minutes.
4. Stir in ½ cup pesto and mix well.
5. Continue simmering, covered, until the rice is fully tender.
6. Mix in the remaining ½ cup pesto and serve warm.

# Potato, Egg, and Tomato Salad

*Serves 6 | Prep. time 20 minutes | Cooking time 20 minutes*

## Ingredients

3 medium vine-ripened tomatoes, chopped into small pieces
2 pounds medium potatoes
6 large eggs, boiled and cooled
¼ cup extra-virgin olive oil
1 teaspoon dried oregano
2 tablespoons fresh basil, chopped
Salt to taste

## Directions

1. Half-fill a large pot with cold water.
2. Add the unpeeled potatoes and boil for about 20 minutes or until the potatoes are tender. Let cool.
3. Add the tomatoes and oil to a large bowl and season with salt. Toss to combine well.
4. Peel the potatoes and cut them into 1-inch pieces. Peel the eggs and cut them into small pieces.
5. Add the potatoes and eggs to the bowl; mix well.
6. Mix in the oregano and basil; add more olive oil as needed. Serve fresh.

# Rustic Orange and Olive Salad

*Serves 4 | Prep. time 15 minutes | Cooking time 0 minutes*

## Ingredients

3–4 tablespoons extra-virgin olive oil
Juice of 1 lemon
4 large oranges
1 large red onion, thinly sliced
¼ cup olives
Ground black pepper and salt to taste
Fresh thyme for serving

### *Directions*

1. In a mixing bowl, combine the oil, lemon juice, salt, and pepper. Mix well and set aside.
2. Slice the oranges into thin slices and arrange them on a platter.
3. Top with thin slices of red onion and the olives.
4. Add the prepared vinaigrette on top. Season with additional salt and pepper if desired. Sprinkle with fresh thyme.

# Cauliflower Olive Salad

*Serves 4 | Prep. time 15–20 minutes | Cooking time 5 minutes*

### Ingredients
1 head cauliflower, cut into small florets
3 carrots, peeled and cut into ½-inch pieces
½ cup black olives, pitted
2–3 tablespoons roasted pine nuts
3 tablespoons extra-virgin olive oil
1 cup white wine vinegar
Ground black pepper and salt to taste
½ cup chopped Italian parsley

### Directions

1. Heat salted water in a cooking pot.
2. Add the cauliflower florets and carrots and boil for 4–5 minutes. Drain the water and transfer the vegetables to a large bowl.
3. Mix in the olives, pine nuts, parsley, vinegar, and oil. Add salt and pepper to taste.
4. Serve fresh or chilled.

# Caesar Salad

*Serves 6 | Prep. time 10 minutes | Cooking time 10 minutes*

## Ingredients

<u>Caesar Salad Dressing</u>

2 small cloves garlic, minced

1 teaspoon anchovy paste

Juice of 1 lemon

1 teaspoon Dijon mustard

1 teaspoon Worcestershire sauce

1 cup mayonnaise

½ cup freshly grated Parmigiano-Reggiano

¼ teaspoon salt

¼ teaspoon freshly ground black pepper

## Croutons

2 tablespoons butter

2 tablespoons extra virgin olive oil

2 cloves garlic, halved

3 cups French or Italian bread, sliced into ½-inch cubes

Salt and pepper

## For salad

½ cup Parmesan cheese, shredded, plus more for topping if desired

2 heads romaine lettuce, torn into bite-sized pieces

### *Directions*

#### For the dressing

1. Whisk together the garlic, anchovy paste, lemon juice, Dijon mustard, and Worcestershire sauce.
2. Add the mayonnaise, Parmigiano-Reggiano, salt, and pepper. Mix well.
3. Taste and adjust the proportions to your liking.
4. Will keep, refrigerated, for 2 weeks.

#### For the croutons

5. Preheat the oven to 350°F.
6. Heat the butter, olive oil, and garlic in a saucepan over low heat.
7. Remove the saucepan from the heat as soon as the butter has melted.
8. Let it stand for 10 minutes, and then remove the garlic.
9. Toss in the bread cubes, and mix to coat.
10. Spread the bread cubes on the baking sheet, and bake until the croutons are golden brown (about 10 minutes), shaking the pan once or twice.
11. Remove the pan from the oven and set it aside to cool.

#### To assemble the salad

12. Toss the lettuce and croutons in the dressing until well coated.
13. Sprinkle on the Parmesan cheese and toss lightly.
14. Sprinkle more Parmesan on top, if desired, and serve.

# Antipasto Salad

*Serves 8 | Prep. time 15 minutes | Cooking time 0 minutes*

## Ingredients

¼ pound Genoa salami, diced

¼ pound pepperoni, diced

2 cups giardiniera (Italian pickled vegetables), coarsely chopped

12 black or Kalamata olives

12 jumbo green olives

1 (8-ounce) jar roasted red peppers, drained and diced

1 (6-ounce) jar marinated artichoke hearts, drained

¼ red onion, sliced

½ cup fresh Mozzarella cubed

¼ cup fresh basil leaves

<u>Dressing</u>
2 tablespoons balsamic vinegar
¼ cup extra-virgin olive oil
Salt, to taste
Freshly ground pepper, to taste

## *Directions*
1. Combine salad ingredients (through red onion) in a bowl.
2. Season with salt and pepper, and then drizzle with olive oil and balsamic vinegar.
3. Toss well.

# Caprese Salad

*Serves 4 | Prep. time 45 minutes | Cooking time 0 minutes*

## Ingredients

4 large tomatoes, sliced ¼ inch thick
1 pound fresh mozzarella, sliced ¼ inch thick
¼ cup packed fresh basil, washed and dried
⅓ teaspoon dried oregano, crumbled
3 tablespoons extra-virgin olive oil
Fine sea salt, to taste
Freshly ground black pepper, to taste

## Directions

1. Layer the tomato and mozzarella slices alternately on a serving dish.
2. Sprinkle with oregano and drizzle with olive oil.
3. Season with salt and pepper.

# PASTA

## Homemade Pasta Dough

*Serves 6 | Prep. time 1 hour 45 min plus | Cooking time 3 minutes*

### Ingredients
1 pound (3 ⅓ cups) all-purpose flour
4 whole eggs plus 1 yolk
¼ cup extra-virgin olive oil
⅛ teaspoon kosher salt
1 to 2 tablespoons water, or as if needed

### *Directions*

1. Pile the flour on a clean dry work surface, in a heap about 8 inches wide.
2. Make a well in the center.
3. Crack all the eggs and then pour the extra yolk into the well and add the olive oil, salt, and water.
4. Using a fork, beat the eggs together with the olive oil, water, and salt. Be careful not to break the sides of the well or the egg mixture will run. You may do this in a bowl, if you fear that the liquid will run all over the work surface.
5. Using the fork, begin to incorporate the flour into the egg mixture. The dough may be lumpy.
6. When liquid ingredients are well incorporated and the mixture is no longer runny, start mixing it with your hands. You can wet your hands first if the dough is dry.
7. When the mixture has become homogeneous, begin kneading on a floured surface. Again, wet your hands if the dough seems too dry and stiff.
8. Use your body weight to stretch and not tear the dough. Use the heels of your palms and knead until it is smooth and velvety (about 8-15 minutes).
9. Wrap the dough in plastic and let it rest for at least 1 hour. It may be refrigerated or frozen for later use.
10. To shape, the dough should be at room temperature.
11. Roll and cut it into the desired shape.
12. To cook, boil in about 6 quarts of water for 1 pound of pasta.
13. Freshly-made pasta will cook in 1-3 minutes.

# Marinara Pasta Sauce

*Serves 6 | Prep. time 20 minutes | Cooking time 35 min to 2 h.*

## Ingredients

8 large fresh tomatoes or 12 Roma tomatoes, seeded and diced into small pieces, OR 2 cans diced tomatoes

½ cup olive oil

8 cloves fresh garlic, minced

¾ cup fresh basil, minced OR 1 tablespoon dried basil

½ teaspoon salt

1 teaspoon fresh ground black pepper

Optional ingredients

¼ teaspoon red pepper flakes, crushed

1 teaspoon sugar

⅛ teaspoon each marjoram and/or oregano

Parmesan cheese

## Directions

1. In a large skillet or saucepan, heat the olive oil over medium heat.
2. Sauté the garlic and cook until it is tender.
3. Add the tomatoes and cook until they are heated through.
4. Stir in the basil and the rest of the ingredients EXCEPT the Parmesan. Simmer until the sauce has the desired thickness (35 minutes for "fresher" sauce or 2 hours for thicker consistency).
5. Serve the sauce over cooked pasta, and sprinkle with Parmesan cheese.

# Creamy Pork Pasta

*Serves 4 | Prep. time 5–8 minutes | Cooking time 25 minutes*

## Ingredients

3 tablespoons olive oil
2 cloves garlic, minced
6 pork sausages, casings removed
¾ cup heavy cream
½ cup dry white wine
¾ pound rigatoni, penne or ziti pasta
¼ cup Parmesan cheese, grated
Salt to taste

## Directions

1. Heat the oil in a medium saucepan or skillet over medium heat.
2. Add in the garlic and sausage; stir-cook to evenly brown and break into small pieces with a wooden spoon.
3. Mix the wine and cook for about 10 minutes.
4. Add the cream, reduce heat to low and cook for 4–5 minutes.
5. Add salted water to a medium saucepan or skillet and heat it over medium heat.
6. Add the pasta and cook as per package directions. Drain water and set aside.
7. Add the pasta to the sausage mix; stir and continue cooking for 1 more minute.
8. Remove from the heat and add the cheese, stirring well. Serve immediately.

# Rustic Fettuccine Pasta

*Serves 4 | Prep. time 10–15 minutes | Cooking time 15 minutes*

## Ingredients

1 (16-ounce) package fettuccine pasta

1 bunch Italian parsley

1 teaspoon lemon juice

½ cup olive oil

6 tablespoons pine nuts

⅓ cup ricotta cheese

½ cup sundried tomatoes, chopped

Ground black pepper and salt as required

1 teaspoon extra-virgin olive oil

Basil leaves for garnish

## Directions

1. Add salted water to a medium saucepan or skillet and heat it over medium heat.
2. Add the pasta and cook as per package directions. Drain water and set aside.
3. Add the parsley, salt, pine nuts, ricotta cheese and lemon juice to a food processor. Season generously with salt and freshly ground black pepper. Blend to make a smooth mixture.
4. Add the ½ cup olive oil while continually running the food processor to make a smooth mixture.
5. Add the pasta to a bowl and top with the parsley mixture and the sundried tomatoes.
6. Toss well and add the 1 teaspoon olive oil; toss again and serve. Garnish with basil leaves.

# Guanciale Pasta Amatriciana

*Serves 6 | Prep. time 10 minutes | Cooking time 55–60 minutes*

### Ingredients

2 (14-ounce) cans whole peeled tomatoes

1 onion, finely chopped

¼ cup olive oil

1 teaspoon crushed red pepper flakes

¼ pound guanciale (pork jowl), finely chopped

¼ pound Italian bacon, finely chopped

¼ cup tomato paste

1 cup dry white wine

1 teaspoon sugar

1 pound penne pasta

Grated Parmesan or pecorino cheese as needed

## Directions

1. Add salted water to a medium saucepan or skillet and heat it over medium-high heat.
2. Add the pasta and cook as per package directions. Drain water and set aside.
3. Puree the tomatoes in a blender.
4. Heat the oil in a medium saucepan or skillet over medium heat.
5. Add the guanciale, onion, pancetta and ½ cup of water; stir-cook the mixture for 8–10 minutes.
6. Mix in the tomato paste and cook for a few minutes.
7. Mix in the wine and cook until the mixture thickens.
8. Mix in the tomato puree; simmer for about 40–45 minutes. Season with salt and pepper.
9. Add the pasta and combine well. Top with the cheese and serve warm.

# Chicken Carbonara Rigatoni

*Serves 6 | Prep. time 15 minutes | Cooking time 4–6 minutes*

## Ingredients

½ cup Parmesan cheese, grated, divided
2 egg yolks, beaten
1 pound rigatoni
½ cup butter, melted
1 cup heavy whipping cream
1 teaspoon salt
Ground pepper to taste
1 pound chicken breasts, cubed

## *Directions*

1. Add salted water to a medium saucepan or skillet and heat it over medium heat.
2. Add the pasta and cook as per package directions. Drain water and set aside.
3. Melt the butter in a medium saucepan or skillet over medium heat.
4. Add chicken and brown the meat until cooked through about 6-8 minutes.
5. Add ¼ cup of the Parmesan cheese as well as the egg yolks, cream, salt, and pepper. Stir with whisk or wooden spoon taking care to release the bits of flavor stuck on the bottom the pan. Cook for about 5 minutes.
6. Mix in the cooked rigatoni and simmer the mixture for 15 minutes, stirring occasionally. Sprinkle with the remaining Parmesan cheese and serve warm.

# Pork Chop Spaghetti

*Serves 4 | Prep. time 10–15 minutes | Cooking time 45–50 minutes*

### Ingredients
4 lean pork chops
1 teaspoon dried rosemary, crumbled
½ teaspoon salt
3 tablespoons extra-virgin olive oil
½ cup butter, melted (divided))
2 large cloves garlic, mashed
¼ teaspoon ground black pepper
⅛ teaspoon crushed red pepper (optional)
2 cups canned peeled Italian tomatoes, chopped
10 Italian parsley sprigs, chopped
¾ pound spaghetti
¼ cup Parmesan cheese, grated

### Directions

1. Add salted water to a medium saucepan or skillet and heat it over medium heat.
2. Add the pasta and cook as per package directions. Drain water and set aside.
3. Heat the oil in a medium saucepan or skillet over medium heat. Add ¼ cup of the butter and melt it.
4. Add the garlic and red pepper; stir-cook for 2–3 minutes to soften until aromatic.
5. Add the pork chops and rosemary; stir-cook for 4–5 minutes to brown on each side. Lower heat to medium and add the salt, tomatoes, and parsley.
6. Stir the mixture, cover and simmer for 20 minutes.
7. Uncover and cook for 20 minutes more, or until cooked well.
8. Mix in the pasta. Add the remaining ¼ cup butter and mix well.
9. Top with the grated Parmesan and serve warm.

# Pancetta Bucatini

*Serves 4 | Prep. time 8–10 minutes | Cooking time 20–25 minutes*

### Ingredients
½ cup dry white wine
1 tablespoon olive oil
½ small onion, finely chopped
1 (28-ounce) can crushed tomatoes
¾ pound bucatini pasta or spaghetti
½ cup pancetta, cubed
½ cup pecorino romano cheese, grated
Salt to taste

## *Directions*

1. Add salted water to a medium saucepan or skillet and heat it over medium heat.
2. Add the pasta and cook as per package directions. Drain water and set aside.
3. In a saucepan or skillet over medium heat, cook the pancetta for several minutes until the fat is rendered. Take out the pancetta and place in a container, leaving the remaining fat in the pan.
4. Add the wine and cook until the alcohol evaporates.
5. Add the oil and onion and cook for several minutes until softened and translucent.
6. Add the tomatoes and pancetta. Stir-cook for 15–18 minutes.
7. Mix in the pasta and cook for 2 additional minutes.
8. Combine well, stir in the cheese and serve warm.

# Pomodoro Spaghetti

*Serves 6 | Prep. time 10–15 minutes | Cooking time 35–40 minutes*

### Ingredients
4½ cups tomatoes, finely chopped

1 onion, roughly chopped

12 basil leaves

1 pound uncooked spaghetti

Parmesan or ricotta salata cheese, finely grated

3 tablespoons extra-virgin olive oil

Salt to taste

## Directions

1. Heat the olive oil in a medium saucepan or skillet over medium heat. Add the onion and stir-fry for 1-2 minutes until soft and fragrant. Add tomatoes and salt. Cook for 25–30 minutes to soften, stir frequently.
2. While the sauce is simmering, cook pasta as per package directions. Drain water and set aside.
3. Crush the tomatoes with a wooden spoon and remove the excess liquid.
4. If desired, transfer the mixture to a blender and blend well to make a smooth sauce.
5. Return sauce to pan to keep warm on low heat, add cooked pasta and warm for a 1-2 minutes on low heat. Add basil leaves.
6. Serve topped with a drizzle of olive oil, if desired, and some grated cheese.

# Pasta Carbonara

*Serves 4 | Prep. time 10 minutes | Cooking time 15 minutes*

## Ingredients

¾ pound spaghetti, linguini, or fettuccini

3 large eggs

6 ounces pancetta or thick-cut bacon, diced or cubed

¼ cup pecorino romano cheese, grated, plus more for sprinkling

3 tablespoons extra-virgin olive oil

Salt to taste

### Directions

1. Add salted water to a medium saucepan or skillet and heat it over medium heat.
2. Add the pasta and cook as per package directions. Drain water and set aside.
3. Whisk the eggs and cheese in a mixing bowl. Mix well and set aside.
4. Add the pancetta/bacon to a medium saucepan or skillet and cook over medium heat for 6–7 minutes, until crisp.
5. Mix in the pasta and olive oil; toss well.
6. Reduce heat to low and add the egg and cheese mixture, stirring constantly.
7. Continue to stir while cooking for 1 minute. Serve with additional cheese on top.

# Fagioli Bean Pasta

*Serves 4 | Prep. time 8–10 minutes | Cooking time 25 minutes*

## Ingredients

1 small onion, chopped

2 cloves garlic, minced

2 tablespoons olive oil

1 teaspoon salt

1½ cups elbow-shaped pasta

2 cups canned crushed tomatoes

1 cup water

2 (16-ounce) cans cannellini beans, drained

### Directions

1. Add salted water to a medium saucepan or skillet and heat it over medium heat.
2. Add the pasta and cook as per package directions. Drain water and set aside.
3. Heat the oil in a medium saucepan or skillet over medium heat.
4. Add the onion, garlic, and salt; stir-cook for 1–2 minutes until soft and translucent.
5. Add the tomatoes and 1 cup of water and simmer over low heat for 16–18 minutes.
6. Add the beans and keep cooking for 5 minutes, stirring continually.
7. Add the cooked pasta and combine well. Serve warm.

# Florentine Fettuccini

*Serves 6 | Prep. time 10 minutes | Cooking time 25–30 minutes*

## Ingredients

¾ pound fettuccine

1¼ cups spinach, chopped

3 tablespoons extra-virgin olive oil

1 small onion, thinly sliced

1½ cups milk

1 pound ricotta cheese

1½ teaspoons salt

Parmesan cheese, grated, for garnish

Freshly ground pepper to taste

## Directions

1. Add salted water to a medium saucepan or skillet and heat it over medium heat.
2. Add the pasta and cook as per package directions. Drain water and set aside.
3. Add the spinach to a medium bowl; pour in boiling water and let stand for 5 minutes.
4. Drain water.
5. Heat the oil in a medium saucepan or skillet over medium heat.
6. Add the onion; stir-cook until soft and translucent, about 1-2 minutes. Add mushrooms and stir-fry until browned.
7. Add the spinach and cook, stirring frequently, until cooked well.
8. Add the cooked fettuccine, ricotta cheese, milk, and salt; cook over low heat while tossing gently for a few minutes, until heated through and sauce has thickened a little, about 5 minutes.
9. Serve warm topped with grated Parmesan cheese and ground pepper, if desired.

# Spaghetti Bolognese

*Serves 6 | Prep: time 20 minutes | Cook time 3 hours*

### Ingredients
Olive oil
1 cup onion, chopped
¾ cup carrot, chopped
½ cup celery, chopped
4 cloves garlic, minced
1 cup mushrooms, sliced
1½ pounds ground veal
¾ cup dry white wine
4 cans (15-ounce) chopped Italian tomatoes (plum), undrained
½ teaspoon salt or to taste
½ teaspoon freshly ground black pepper
1 teaspoon dried oregano

2 bay leaves
1 teaspoon dried thyme
½ teaspoon dried basil
⅛ teaspoon nutmeg
¼ teaspoon white pepper
1 pound Spaghetti
Parmesan shavings

### *Directions*

1. Add about 2 tablespoons olive oil into a Dutch oven or a large covered pot. Over medium heat, cook the onion, carrot, and celery, about 4 minutes or until softened. Stir in mushrooms and garlic, and cook an additional 4–5 minutes. Add ground veal, and cook until meat is browned.
2. Add wine, and bring mixture to a boil. Reduce heat and add all remaining ingredients. Cover, and cook over low heat 2 ½ to 3 hours, stirring occasionally.
3. Serve over freshly cooked spaghetti pasta. Sprinkle with shaved Parmesan if desired.

# Linguine with Seafood in Tomato Sauce

*Serves 6 | Prep: time 15 minutes | Cook time 20 minutes*

## Ingredients

18 small littleneck clams

½ pound calamari, cleaned and cut into ¼ inch rings

4 tablespoons extra-virgin olive oil

2 teaspoons garlic, minced

2 tablespoons fresh parsley, chopped

2 cups ripe tomatoes, peeled and chopped (retain juice)

1 tablespoon sugar

½ cup white wine

1 tablespoon lemon zest

½ lemon, juiced

1 tablespoon red chili pepper, minced

Sea salt and freshly ground black pepper

1 pound linguine pasta

## *Directions*

1. Wash and scrub the clams well. Discard any that are open. Place in a wide pan no more than 3-inch deep. Add about 1½ inch of water. Cover and turn the heat on high. Cook until clams open up, about 10 minutes. Turn them over once as they cook and remove each one as it opens. Remove clams from shells and set aside. Carefully spoon up ½ cup of the cooking liquid and reserve.
2. Cook linguine according to package directions.
3. In a skillet, over medium-high heat, add olive oil, and garlic. Cook garlic about 2 minutes. Reduce heat to medium, and add tomatoes, sugar, wine, lemon zest, chili, and reserved cooking liquid. Cook 2–3 minutes until tomatoes are soft. Taste the sauce and adjust seasoning with salt and pepper to taste. Add calamari, and cook for 2-3 minutes more until tender.
4. Serve by placing pasta on serving platter, then the calamari tomato sauce and clams. Add the juice half a lemon and stir. To serve, sprinkle with Parmesan cheese grated over top and parsley.

# Gnocchi Basic Recipe

*Serves 6 | Prep time 30 minutes | Cook time 35 minutes*

### Ingredients
1½ pounds boiling potatoes (do not substitute new potatoes; they do not have the same starch level required)
1 ½ cups all-purpose flour
Olive oil

### Directions
1. Boil the potatoes, skins on, in a large pot of water until tender, about 30 minutes. Drain.

2. As soon as you can touch them, remove the skins from hot potatoes. Press the potatoes through a food mill, and turn onto the counter. Add most of the flour, and begin to knead. When the mixture is smooth and soft, but still sticky, there is enough flour.
3. Roll dough out into 1-inch-thick logs. Slice into ¾-inch pieces dusting hands and knife with flour as needed. Next, shape the gnocchi by rolling each along a fork, creating grooves. They should become barrel-shaped. Continue until all have been rolled.
4. To cook: boil 4 quarts of water in a large, wide pot to which about a tablespoon of olive oil has been added. Drop gnocchi, in batches, and cook for just 8–10 seconds, scooping out with a slotted spoon. Transfer to serving plate and keep warm.

# Gnocchi Piedmont Style

*Serves 6 | Prep. time 15 minutes | Cook time 25 minutes*

### Ingredients
1 batch gnocchi, cooked
4 cups tomato sauce
1 cup fresh mushrooms, sliced
½ cup prosciutto, chopped
1 tablespoon butter
2 green onions, chopped
1 cup heavy cream (35% fat)
¼ teaspoon nutmeg
½ teaspoon freshly ground black pepper
⅓ cup Parmesan cheese, freshly grated
¼ cup fresh parsley, chopped

## Directions

1. Melt butter in a saucepan over medium heat. Add mushrooms, prosciutto, onions, and cook until softened. Stir in cream, pepper, and nutmeg, and heat to boiling. Reduce heat and cook, uncovered, until thickened, about 15 minutes. Stir frequently.
2. Stir in spaghetti sauce, and simmer an additional 10–12 minutes until heated through.
3. Serve over hot gnocchi. Sprinkle with Parmesan and chopped parsley.

# Shells Pasta with Ham and Peas

*Serves 4 | Prep. time 10 minutes | Cook time 15 minutes*

## Ingredients

2 cups small shell macaroni, cooked

1 tablespoon butter

½ cup onion, minced

4 ounces ham, cut into bite-sized strips

2 tablespoons all-purpose flour

1 cup peas, cooked (fresh or frozen)

1 cup half and half

¼ cup fresh Parmesan cheese, grated

## *Directions*

1. While pasta and peas are cooking, dice onion and ham.
2. Heat butter in a medium saucepan over medium heat. Add the onion, and cook until translucent, about 4–5 minutes. Add the ham, and stir to heat through. Add the flour and mix well. Slowly add the half and half, stirring constantly, and bring to a boil. Reduce heat, and add the peas. Cook until just thickened.
3. To serve, pour sauce over cooked pasta, and sprinkle with Parmesan cheese.

# Classic Lasagna

*Serves 10 | preparation time 1 hour 35 min. | Cooking time 30 min.*

### Ingredients
16 flat "no boil" lasagna noodles
4 cups mozzarella cheese, grated, divided

For meat sauce
1 large yellow onion, chopped
1 tablespoon olive oil
2 cloves garlic, peeled and minced
1 pound ground beef, preferably sirloin
1 pound ground Italian sausage
1 teaspoon kosher salt
1 tablespoon dried basil

1 tablespoon dried oregano

1 tablespoon dried parsley

12 ounces tomato paste

1 (28-ounce) can whole San Marzano tomatoes

¼ cup red wine or water


For cheese sauce

3 cups whole milk ricotta

2 eggs

2 tablespoons fresh parsley, chopped

½ teaspoon freshly ground black pepper

½ cup Parmesan cheese, freshly grated


### *Directions*

For the meat sauce

1. Sauté the onion in olive oil over medium heat in a medium-sized pot.
2. Add the garlic, beef, and sausage and cook, with stirring, until browned.
3. Stir in the salt, basil, parsley, and oregano.
4. Stir in the tomato paste.
5. Scoop out the San Marzano tomatoes one by one, crushing each with your hand over the sauce to catch the juice. Drop the crushed tomato into the sauce as well.
6. Swirl the wine or water in the can to get remaining tomato juice and pour it into the pot. Stir, and reduce the heat to low.
7. Cover and let simmer for 45 minutes.


For the cheese sauce

8. In a large bowl, mix ricotta, eggs, parsley, black pepper, and Parmesan together.
9. Keep refrigerated until ready to assemble lasagna.


To assemble the lasagna

10. Preheat the oven to 375°F and grease a 13x9 baking pan.
11. Spread 1 cup of meat sauce on the bottom of the baking pan.
12. Arrange 4 lasagna noodles in a layer over the meat sauce.
13. Spread ⅓ of the cheese sauce on top, and sprinkle with about ½ cup of mozzarella
14. Continue layering, ending with meat sauce sprinkled with mozzarella.
15. Bake the lasagna until the cheese is golden (about 30-40 minutes).
16. Let sit for 10 minutes before serving.

# Lasagna with Bechamel Sauce

Serves 8 | Prep. time 20 min. | *Cook time 55 min.* | *Resting time 15 min.*

## Ingredients for the bechamel

5 tablespoons butter
4 tablespoons all-purpose flour
4 cups milk
1 teaspoon salt
½ teaspoon black pepper, freshly ground
¼ teaspoon nutmeg, freshly grated
½ cup Parmesan cheese, freshly grated

## Directions

1. Heat butter in a saucepan over medium heat until melted. Stir in flour to make a roux, and whisk until light golden brown, about 7 minutes.
2. Meanwhile, heat the milk in a separate pan. Do not boil. Add the hot milk to the flour, a cup at a time, whisking continuously until smooth. Cook 10 minutes whisking constantly. Remove from heat. Add black pepper to taste, and nutmeg. Stir in Parmesan cheese.

## Ingredients for the tomato sauce

2 (32-ounce) cans whole tomatoes
3 tablespoons butter, unsalted
1 tablespoon olive oil
½ small onion diced
3 cloves garlic, minced
1 rib celery, chopped
1 carrot, chopped
4 basil leaves
1 bay leave
Sea salt and freshly ground black pepper

## Directions

1. In a large pot, melt butter and add onion. Sauté for about 2-3 minutes until translucent. Add garlic, celery, and carrot, and cook about 5 minutes more. Add tomatoes, basil, and bay leaf.
2. Cover and simmer over low heat for about an hour. Run the sauce through a food processor when done cooking to eliminate any vegetable chunks. Salt and pepper to taste.

## Ingredients for the lasagna

12 lasagna noodles
1 pound ground turkey, browned
1 pound mozzarella, shredded
8 ounces Parmesan, grated
Bechamel sauce
Tomato sauce

## Directions

1. Preheat oven to 350ºF. Lightly oil a 9" x 13" baking pan. Cook lasagna noodles according to package directions.
2. To assemble the lasagna, begin with 1 layer of pasta on the bottom of the oiled dish. You will be making 4 layers, so divide the ingredients proportionately. Next add the red sauce, béchamel sauce, Parmesan, and mozzarella. Repeat 3 times, ending with cheese on top. Cover and bake lasagna 30 minutes. Allow to rest 15 minutes prior to serving.

# Creamy Walnut Pesto Sauce on Penne

*Serves 6 | Prep. time 10 minutes | Cook time 10 minutes*

### Ingredients
1 pound linguini pasta
3 cups basil leaves
¼ cup fresh parsley leaves
1 cup walnuts
3 tablespoons garlic, minced
1 cup olive oil
1 cup Parmesan cheese
Coarse ground salt

Freshly ground black pepper
½ cup whipping cream

### *Directions*

1. Boil pasta according to package directions.
2. In a food processor, combine basil, parsley, walnuts, and garlic until well chopped. With processor running, drizzle olive oil in a slow stream.
3. Add the cheese, salt, and pepper. Adjust salt and pepper to taste. Pour in whipping cream. Serve over hot pasta.

# Linguine Primavera

*Serves 6 | Prep. time 10 minutes | Cook time 20 minutes*

## *Ingredients*

½ pound linguine
Olive oil
1 crown of broccoli, chopped
½ pound asparagus
1 portabella mushroom
1 medium zucchini, sliced lengthwise in halved
1 cup roasted red peppers, chopped
1 cup peas, fresh or thawed
2 cloves garlic, minced
1 shallot, minced
¾ cup white wine

1 cup chicken stock
2 tablespoons butter
½ cup Parmesan cheese, freshly grated
3 tablespoons fresh basil, chopped
3 tablespoons fresh parsley, chopped
Sea salt and freshly ground black pepper

## *Directions*

1. Preheat grill to medium. Brush olive oil on broccoli, asparagus, mushroom, and zucchini. When the grill is hot, cook vegetables until charred, turning occasionally. Remove from heat and dice into bite-sized pieces. This can also be done in the oven at 400⁰F on a baking sheet for 20-25 minutes
2. In a small saucepan, combine shallots, garlic, wine, and chicken stock. Bring to a boil and cook 10–12 minutes. Remove from heat, and stir in butter until melted, then Parmesan cheese, and stir until melted.
3. Cook the linguine according to package directions. Meanwhile, place all vegetables in a mixing bowl. Toss with wine sauce, salt, and pepper. When linguine is finished, toss with dressed vegetables and serve.

# Spaghetti with Meatballs

*Serves 6 | preparation 15 minutes | Cooking time 45 minutes*

## Ingredients

2 (30-ounce) jars of spaghetti sauce or 3 ¾ cups marinara pasta sauce (p53)
1 pound spaghetti, cooked al dente

For meatballs
2 pounds lean ground beef
2 eggs
¾ cup dry bread crumbs
¼ cup fresh parsley, chopped
2 garlic cloves, minced
½ teaspoon salt or to taste
¼ cup Parmesan cheese

### *Directions*

1. Combine the meatball ingredients in a bowl, mixing thoroughly.
2. Shape the mixture into 18 meatballs.
3. In a saucepan, bring the sauce to a simmer.
4. Add meatballs and return to a simmer.
5. Cover and cook until the meatballs are cooked through (about 35-40 minutes).
6. Serve the sauce and meatballs over warm spaghetti.

# Fettucine Alfredo

*Serves 4 | preparation time 5 minutes | Cooking time 15 minutes*

## Ingredients

8-ounce package fettuccine, cooked according to packaging instructions and drained
¼ cup water, reserved from cooking pasta
3 tablespoons unsalted butter
1 small shallot, finely minced
½ cup heavy cream
¾ cup freshly Parmigiano-Reggiano or Parmesan, grated
¼ teaspoon salt
Freshly ground black pepper, to taste

For garnish
Fresh basil
Parmigiano-Reggiano or Parmesan, grated

### Directions

1. Melt the butter in a deep frying pan or heavy-bottomed pot over medium-high heat.
2. Sauté the shallots until tender, about 2 minutes.
3. Add the cream and bring to a low boil.
4. Reduce the heat to medium-low and simmer for 3 minutes.
5. Remove the pan from the heat and stir in the cheese, salt, and pepper until smooth.
6. Add the cooked pasta and reserved pasta water to the sauce.
7. Return the pan to the stove over medium-high heat, and gently stir the pasta in the sauce to coat.
8. Garnish with Parmigiano-Reggiano and fresh basil, and serve.

# Creamy Pesto Linguini

*Serves 6 | Prep. time 10 minutes | Cooking time 3 minutes*

## Ingredients

⅓ cup extra-virgin olive oil

½ cup heavy cream

2 tablespoons butter

1 (12-ounce) pack linguine pasta, cooked according to packaging instructions and drained

Pesto Sauce

¾ cup fresh basil leaves

¾ cup grated Parmesan cheese, divided

3 tablespoons pine nuts

2 cloves garlic, peeled

½ teaspoon kosher salt

½ teaspoon freshly ground pepper

**Directions**

1. To make the pesto, combine the basil, ½ cup of Parmesan cheese, pine nuts, garlic, salt, and pepper in a food processor. Pulse to combine.
2. Add the oil gradually, in drizzles, while processing.
3. In a saucepan, combine the butter and cream over medium heat.
4. Add the pesto to the cream mixture and stir, simmering for 3 minutes.
5. Remove from the heat, add the remaining Parmesan, and stir well.
6. Lastly, add the drained linguine and mix well.

# Seafood Linguini Alla Vongole

*Serves 4 | Prep. time 15 minutes | Cooking time 15 minutes*

## Ingredients

2 ¼ pounds mixed shellfish (like clams, mussels, scampi, unpeeled shrimp or prawns), cleaned

¼ cup dry white wine

25-30 cherry tomatoes, halved, seeded, and juiced

1 (16-ounce) pack dried linguine, cooked according to packaging directions, drained

½ cup olive oil

5 garlic cloves, thinly sliced

⅛ teaspoon dried chili flakes, or to taste

3 tablespoons flat leaf parsley, chopped

Salt and freshly ground black pepper, to taste

## *Directions*

1. Start with the clams and mussels. After cleaning, put them in a pot with the wine.
2. Cover and cook over high heat until the shells have opened (about 4 minutes). Remove unopened shellfish and discard. Set aside the opened clams and shellfish. Reserve all but about 2 tablespoons of the cooking liquid.
3. Chop the seeded, squeezed cherry tomatoes.
4. Meanwhile, put the olive oil and garlic into a large pan, and heat gently until the garlic begins to sizzle.
5. Add the chili flakes and chopped tomatoes, and simmer for 5 minutes.
6. Add the strained, reserved liquid from the clams and bring it again to a boil.
7. Simmer until the liquid is reduced.
8. Add the scampi into the sauce and cook until pink in color, flipping over once.
9. Add the prawns and simmer until cooked (about 3 minutes).
10. Stir in the cooked clams and mussels.
11. Add the parsley and continue cooking, turning over seafood occasionally, until heated through.
12. Season with a little salt and pepper, as desired.
13. Pour over cooked pasta and toss.

# Shrimp Pasta in Spicy Tomato Sauce

*Serves 4 | Prep. time 15 minutes | Cooking time 18 minutes*

### Ingredients

1 pound large shrimp, peeled and deveined

1 teaspoon salt, or as needed

1 teaspoon dried crushed red pepper flakes

4-5 tablespoons olive oil, divided

1 medium onion, sliced

1 (14.5-ounce) can diced tomatoes, juice retained

1 cup dry white wine

3 cloves garlic, chopped

¼ teaspoon dried oregano leaves

3 tablespoon fresh Italian parsley leaves, chopped

3 tablespoon fresh basil leaves, chopped

Cooked pasta for serving

## Directions

1. In a bowl, mix together the shrimp, salt, and red pepper flakes.
2. Heat 3 tablespoons of oil in a large skillet over medium-high heat.
3. Add shrimp and sauté until just cooked through (about 2 minutes). Place it in a dish and set it aside.
4. Using the same skillet, sauté the onion in 1 to 2 teaspoons of olive oil until translucent (about 5 minutes).
5. Add the undrained tomatoes, wine, garlic, and oregano.
6. Simmer until the sauce begins to thicken (about 10 minutes)
7. Return the shrimp and its juices to the tomato mixture.
8. Toss and cook about 1 minute longer.
9. Stir in the parsley, basil, and more salt as needed. Serve over pasta.

# Spicy Shrimp Pasta All'Arrabbiata

*Serves 4 | Prep. time 10 minutes | Cooking time 20 minutes*

## Ingredients

1 ½ pounds large shrimp, peeled and deveined
½ teaspoon salt
1 teaspoon red pepper flakes
½ teaspoon cayenne pepper
¼ cup olive oil
½ cup onion, chopped
½ green pepper, diced
2 cans whole tomatoes (14 ounces)
1 cup white wine
4 cloves garlic, sliced

½ teaspoon dried oregano

1 anchovy, rinsed and minced (optional, but recommended)

1 red chili, chopped

1 teaspoon freshly ground black pepper

1 tablespoon extra-virgin olive oil

Cooked pasta for serving

## *Directions*

1. In a mixing bowl, toss shrimp with salt and pepper flakes and cayenne and set aside.
2. Cook pasta according to package directions.
3. Heat oil in a large skillet. Cook shrimp in olive oil for two minutes, and remove from pan.
4. To the same skillet, add onion and peppers, and cook until translucent, about 5 minutes. Next, add tomatoes, wine, garlic, oregano, anchovy, and red chili. Cook about 9–12 minutes until sauce thickens slightly. Adjust salt and pepper to taste. Return shrimp to pan, add olive oil and stir to coat. Remove from heat.
5. To serve, add hot pasta to dishes, top with sauce and stir to combine.

# Pasta Alla Puttanesca

*Serves 4 | Prep. time 10 minutes | Cooking time 25 minutes*

### Ingredients

1 (14-ounce) package spaghetti, cooked according to packaging instructions, drained
2 tablespoons olive oil
2 cloves garlic, chopped
1 small red chili, finely chopped
1 cup pitted black olives, sliced
6 sundried tomatoes, cut into thin strips
2 anchovy fillets, chopped (optional)
2 tablespoons salted capers, rinsed
1 (14.5-ounce) can diced tomatoes
½ cup fresh basil leaves, shredded
Grated Parmesan, to serve

## *Directions*

1. Heat the olive oil in a skillet over medium heat, and sauté the garlic and chili for 1 minute.
2. Add the olives, sundried tomatoes, capers, anchovies, and diced tomatoes, and simmer for 20 minutes. Season with pepper.
3. Add the pasta to the sauce, and season with basil.
4. Mix well.
5. Serve with Parmesan, if desired.

# Lemon Parmesan Spaghetti

*Serves 4 | Prep. time 8–10 minutes | Cooking time 20 minutes*

### Ingredients
1 cup heavy cream
Juice and zest from 1 large lemon
1 pound spaghetti or spaghettini (thin spaghetti)
¼ cup brandy
¾ cup Parmesan cheese, grated

### Directions
1. Add salted water to a medium saucepan or skillet and heat it over medium heat.
2. Add the pasta and cook as per package directions. Drain water and set aside.
3. In the same saucepan, heat the heavy cream, brandy and lemon juice over low heat.
4. Boil the mixture over high heat for 7–8 minutes until it thickens.
5. Mix in the spaghetti and lemon zest and toss well.
6. Add the cheese; toss again. Serve warm topped with reserved lemon zest.

# RISOTTO

## Mushroom Risotto

*Serves 4 | Prep. time 10 minutes | Cooking time 45 minutes*

### Ingredients

1 tablespoon olive oil
3 small onions, finely chopped
1 garlic clove, crushed
1 teaspoon fresh parsley, minced
1 teaspoon celery, minced
1½ cups button or mini bella mushrooms, sliced
1 cup whole milk
¼ cup heavy cream
1 cup arborio rice, uncooked

5 cups vegetable stock
1 teaspoon butter, melted
1 cup Parmesan cheese, grated
Salt and ground black pepper to taste

### Directions
1. Heat the oil in a medium saucepan or skillet over medium heat.
2. Add the onion and garlic; stir-cook until soft and translucent.
3. Discard the garlic clove and mix in the salt, parsley, celery, and pepper.
4. Stir-cook until the celery becomes softened.
5. Add the mushrooms and reduce the heat to low; stir-cook until the mushrooms become soft.
6. Mix in the rice, cream, and milk.
7. Heat the mixture and add the stock; combine and cook until the rice is cooked well.
8. Mix in the butter and Parmesan cheese; serve warm.

# Scampi Shrimp Risotto

*Serves 6 | Prep. time 10–15 minutes | Cooking time 45–50 minutes*

## Ingredients

2 pounds shrimp, shelled and deveined
½ cup all-purpose flour
½ cup tomato paste
3 tablespoons olive oil
3 onions, sliced thin
Juice of ½ lemon
1½ cups arborio or carnaroli rice, uncooked
1 quart water
3 tablespoons butter
⅓ cup parsley, chopped
Salt and black pepper to taste

## Directions

1. Add the flour and shrimp to a bowl. Coat well and set aside.
2. Heat the oil in a medium saucepan or skillet over medium heat.
3. Add the shrimp and stir-cook to evenly fry.
4. Drain over paper towels and set aside.
5. To the same saucepan or skillet, add the onions and tomato paste.
6. Stir and simmer slowly for 30 minutes.
7. Add the shrimp and lemon juice and stir. Remove from heat and set aside.
8. Add the rice and water to a large saucepan.
9. Bring to a boil and then reduce heat.
10. Stirring frequently, cook until the rice is cooked well and all liquid is absorbed.
11. Transfer the rice to a serving dish. Mix in the butter, parsley, salt, and pepper.
12. Top with the shrimp mixture. Stir gently and serve.

# Northern Italian Risotto

*Serves 4 | Prep. time 15–20 minutes | Cooking time 25–30 minutes*

## Ingredients

3 tablespoons butter

1 onion, chopped

2 cloves garlic, minced

2 tablespoons olive oil

1 cup arborio or carnaroli rice, uncooked

3 cups chicken broth
1 medium carrot, finely diced or grated
½ cup frozen peas, thawed
1 cup Parmesan, romano or asiago cheese, grated
Black pepper and salt to taste
Black olives and lemon slices for garnish

## *Directions*

1. In a large cooking pot, melt the butter over medium heat.
2. Add the olive oil and sauté the onion and garlic until softened and golden.
3. Add the rice and cook, stirring constantly, for 3–4 minutes or until opaque.
4. Add 1 cup of the broth. Stir the mixture.
5. Add the remaining broth and stir-cook until all broth is absorbed.
6. Stir in the salt, black pepper, peas, carrots, and cheese.
7. Serve warm and garnish with black olives and lemon slices if desired.

# Veneto Peas Risotto

*Serves 4 | Prep. time 10 minutes | Cooking time 25 minutes*

## Ingredients

½ small onion, diced
3 tablespoons olive oil

¼ cup pancetta, diced
1½ cups arborio rice
1 quart vegetable broth
1½ cup frozen peas, thawed
½ cup Parmesan cheese, grated
Salt to taste

### *Directions*
1.  Heat the oil in a medium saucepan or skillet over medium heat.
2.  Add the onion; stir-cook for 5 minutes until soft and translucent.
3.  Add the pancetta and stir-cook for 2 minutes.
4.  Add the rice and cook for about 1 minute.
5.  Stir in 2 cups of the broth and continue cooking on medium-low heat for about 10 minutes.
6.  Add the peas, salt, and remaining broth; stir-cook until the rice is creamy and tender, about 10 minutes more.
7.  Stir in the cheese and serve warm.

# Risotto Milanese

*Serves 6 | Prep. time 10 minutes | Cooking time 30–35 minutes*

### Ingredients
2 shallots, minced
1 clove garlic, minced
3 tablespoons olive oil
2 cups Arborio rice
½ cup dry white wine
6 cups chicken stock
½ teaspoon saffron threads
1 cup fresh Parmesan, grated finely, room temperature
4 tablespoons butter
Freshly ground black pepper

***Directions***

1. In a large saucepan, cook the shallots and garlic in olive oil until translucent, about 4–5 minutes. Stir in the rice, and cook an additional 3 minutes. Add the wine, 2 cups of the stock, and saffron threads. Bring to a simmer over medium heat. Cook until most of the liquid is absorbed, stirring often.
2. Add 1 cup of broth at a time, stirring often. When each cup is mostly incorporated, add additional cup. Repeat until rice is completely cooked.
3. Remove from heat, and stir in the Parmesan and 4 tablespoons of butter. Add freshly ground black pepper to taste.

# Four Cheese Risotto

*Serves 4 | Prep. time 10 minutes | Cooking time 25–30 minutes*

### Ingredients

2 tablespoons olive oil
½ cup onion, finely chopped
1 cup Arborio rice
2 tablespoons dry white wine
3–4  cups chicken broth
½ cup ricotta cheese
¼ cup mozzarella, shredded
¼ cup blue cheese (or gorgonzola)

¼ cup Parmesan, grated

1 tablespoon fresh parsley, chopped

## *Directions*

1. Heat oil in a large saucepan over medium heat. Cook onion until tender and translucent, about 5 minutes. Stir in rice, and cook 3–4 minutes, stirring. Add wine, and cook until liquid evaporates.
2. Start with half cup of broth poured over rice mixture. Stir often while cooking. When liquid has evaporated, repeat 1 cup at a time. When rice is creamy and softened, remove from heat and stir in all cheeses. Sprinkle with parsley prior to serving.

# Risotto with Porcini Mushrooms

*Serves 6 | Prep. time 10 minutes | Cooking time 45–50 minutes*

**Ingredients**

2 cups beef broth, diluted with 2 cups water

2 tablespoons butter

2 tablespoons olive oil

2 tablespoons shallot, finely diced

1 clove garlic, finely diced

2 cups Arborio rice

1 package dry porcini mushrooms, about 1 ounce

Freshly ground black pepper

⅓ cup Parmesan, freshly grated

## Directions

1. Soak the mushrooms in 2 cups of warm water, about 30 minutes, to reconstitute. Squeeze mushrooms into the soaking juice once or twice while soaking. Remove from liquid. Strain liquid through a paper towel to remove any bits of dirt. Reserve. Chop mushrooms.

2. In a large pot, bring the broth to a simmer. Meanwhile, sauté shallot and garlic in half the butter and olive oil, about 5 minutes. Add the rice, and stir to coat. Add the first half cup of beef broth, stirring often. After 10 minutes, add the mushrooms and 1 cup of the soaking water. Cook until liquid has evaporated. Add second half of soaking liquid. Repeat the process until all water and broth has been incorporated, and rice is tender.

3. Remove from heat and season with pepper. Add 1 tablespoon butter and Parmesan cheese. Adjust salt to taste and serve.

# PIZZA

## Basic Pizza Dough

*Serves 2 crusts, medium to large in size | Prep. time 2 hours 10 minutes |*
*Cooking time 6-8 minutes (pre-baking)*

### Ingredients
1 tablespoon sugar
1 ⅓ cups warm water (105°F)
1 (0.25-ounce) packet active dry yeast (2 ¼ teaspoons)
3 tablespoons extra-virgin olive oil, plus more for brushing
3 ¾ cups all-purpose flour, plus more for dusting
1 ½ teaspoons salt

### *Directions*

1. Dissolve the sugar in warm water, and add the yeast. Let it sit until the water becomes frothy (about 10 minutes). Stir-in the olive oil.
2. In a large bowl, mix the flour and salt together.
3. Make a well in the center and pour in the yeast mixture.
4. Using a wooden spoon, mix until a rough dough is formed.
5. Place the dough on a floured surface and knead until it becomes smooth and elastic (about 5 minutes).
6. Prepare two bowls and brush them with olive oil.
7. Divide the dough in half as equally as possible (about 1 pound per piece).
8. Place each portion of dough in a prepared bowl, and brush the surface with oil.
9. Cover with plastic wrap and allow the dough to expand to double its size (about 1 hour and 30 minutes).
10. Roll out into desired shape and diameter. The dough may be covered with plastic wrap and stored, frozen, for 1 month.
11. If the pre-baking crust is required, bake at 425°F until lightly browned (about 6-8 minutes).

# Homemade Pizza Sauce

*Yields about 2 cups | Prep. time 15 minutes | Cooking time 1 hours 10 minutes*

### Ingredients

1 (28-ounce) can whole peeled tomatoes

1 tablespoon extra-virgin olive oil

1 tablespoon unsalted butter

2 medium cloves garlic, grated

2 anchovy fillets (optional)

1 teaspoon dried oregano

Pinch red pepper flakes

⅛ teaspoon kosher salt, or to taste

2 sprigs fresh basil, leaves attached

1 medium yellow onion, peeled and halved

1 teaspoon sugar

⅛ cup red wine (optional)

## Directions

1. Make the tomatoes into a chunky (not smooth) consistency using a blender, food processor or food mill. Set aside.
2. Heat the oil and butter over low to medium heat in a saucepan.
3. When the butter has melted, add the garlic, anchovy (optional), oregano, pepper flakes, and salt. If using anchovies, mash them with a wooden spoon or with a fork as you sauté.
4. Stir while cooking until the garlic has browned slightly (about 3-4 minutes).
5. Add the chopped tomatoes, basil, onion, sugar, and red wine (optional).
6. Simmer, stirring occasionally, over very low heat until reduced by ½ (about 1 hour).
7. Remove the onion and basil stems.
8. Adjust the flavor with salt or more pepper flakes, according to taste.
9. Allow to cool to room temperature.
10. Will keep in the refrigerator for 2 weeks.

# Prosciutto Cheese Pizza

*Serves 6 | Prep. time 2 hours | Cooking time 15 minutes*

**Ingredients**

Pizza Dough

¾ cup lukewarm water

2½ cups all-purpose flour

1½ teaspoons salt

2 teaspoons quick yeast

Olive oil as required

Pizza

¼ cup tomato sauce

1 cup mozzarella cheese, shredded

½ teaspoon dried thyme

2 teaspoons garlic powder

6 ounces thinly sliced prosciutto

### Directions

<u>Dough</u>

1. Combine the water and yeast in a bowl and whisk well. Set aside for about 5 minutes.
2. Add the flour and salt. Combine the mixture until a soft dough forms.
3. Place it over a floured surface and knead for a few minutes to form a ball-shaped dough.
4. Place the dough in an olive-oil-greased bowl.
5. Cover with plastic wrap.
6. Set aside to rise at room temperature for 1½ to 2 hours.
7. Divide into 2 dough rounds and use as required.

<u>Pizza</u>

1. Grease a 10-inch pizza pan with olive oil.
2. Place a prepared pizza dough round in the pizza pan. Stretch the dough to cover the pan surface evenly.
3. Preheat the oven to 400°F.
4. Spread the tomato sauce evenly over the dough, leaving a ½-inch border.
5. Sprinkle the garlic powder and thyme evenly. Top with the cheese and lastly add the prosciutto on top.
6. Bake for 12–15 minutes or until golden and crisp.
7. Slice and serve warm.

# Sausage Arugula Pizza

*Serves 6 | Prep. time 20 minutes | Cooking time 12 minutes*

## *Ingredients*

Dough

¾ cup lukewarm water

2½ cups all-purpose flour

1½ teaspoons salt

2 teaspoons quick yeast

Olive oil as required

Pizza

¼ cup unsalted tomato sauce

½-1 cup mozzarella cheese, shredded

½ teaspoon dried thyme

2 teaspoons garlic powder

¼ pound Italian sausages, cooked and sliced

1 cup arugula, chopped

Olive oil as required

## *Directions*

Dough

1. Combine the water and yeast in a bowl; whisk well. Set aside for about 5 minutes.
2. Add the flour and salt and combine the mixture until a soft dough forms.
3. Place it over a floured surface and knead for a few minutes to form a ball-shaped dough.
4. Place the dough in an olive-oil-greased bowl.
5. Cover with plastic wrap.
6. Set aside to rise at room temperature for 1½ to 2 hours.
7. Divide into 2 dough rounds and use as required.

Pizza

1. Grease a 10-inch pizza pan with olive oil.
2. Place a prepared pizza dough round in the pizza pan. Stretch the dough to cover the pan surface evenly.
3. Preheat the oven to 400°F.
4. Spread the tomato sauce evenly over the dough, leaving a ½-inch border.
5. Sprinkle the garlic powder and thyme evenly. Top with the mozzarella cheese and lastly add the sausage on top.
6. Bake for 12–15 minutes or until golden and crisp.
7. Top with the chopped arugula and some olive oil; bake for 30 seconds more.
8. Slice and serve warm.

# Classic Marinara Pizza

*Serves 6 | Prep. time 15–20 minutes | Cooking time 20 minutes*

### Ingredients

<u>Dough:</u>

¾ cup lukewarm water

2½ cups all-purpose flour

1½ teaspoons salt

2 teaspoons quick yeast

Olive oil as required

<u>Pizza:</u>

1 pizza dough round

1½ cups canned crushed tomatoes

1 large clove garlic, thinly sliced
1 teaspoon dried oregano
Olive oil to taste
Ground black pepper to taste

### *Directions*

Dough:

1. Combine the water and yeast in a bowl; whisk well. Set aside for about 5 minutes.
2. Add the flour and salt and combine the mixture until a soft dough forms.
3. Place it over a floured surface and knead for a few minutes to form a ball-shaped dough.
4. Place the dough in an olive-oil-greased bowl.
5. Cover with plastic wrap.
6. Set aside to rise at room temperature for 1½ to 2 hours.
7. Divide into 2 dough rounds and use as required.

Pizza:

1. Grease one 8–10-inch pizza pan with olive oil.
2. Place a prepared pizza dough round in the pizza pan. Stretch the dough to cover the pan surface evenly.
3. Preheat the oven to 400°F / 204°C.
4. Spread the tomatoes evenly over the dough, leaving a ½-inch border.
5. Top with the garlic, oregano, black pepper, and some olive oil.
6. Bake for 15–18 minutes or until golden and crisp.
7. Slice and serve warm.

# Sicilian Pizza

*Serves 8 | Prep. time 15 minutes | Cooking time 10 minutes*

## Ingredients

1 rectangular pan pizza crust

½ cup marinara sauce

1 pound mozzarella cheese, sliced thinly

12 ounces pepperoni, sliced thinly

4 ounces ground Pecorino Romano cheese, divided

Fresh basil leaves (optional)

## Directions

1. Preheat oven to 550°F.
2. Arrange the mozzarella slices so that dough is covered evenly.
3. Spread marinara sauce over cheese.
4. Cover with pepperoni slices and sprinkle with half of the ground cheese.
5. Bake until crust is browned and pepperoni look crisp, about 10 minutes. Lift slightly to check the bottom of crust (It should be golden brown).
6. Sprinkle with remaining cheese and serve immediately.

# Stuffed Crust Pizza

*Serves 8 | Prep. time 25 min. | Rest time 20 -35 min. | Cooking time 20-25 min.*

## Ingredients

3 cups all-purpose flour
½ teaspoon salt
1 tablespoon sugar
¾ ounce (1 packet) instant dry yeast
1 cup lukewarm water
2 tablespoons olive oil
⅛ cup cornmeal (or all-purpose flour)
Mozzarella, shredded
Favorite toppings

## *Directions*

1. Whisk flour and salt together.
2. Whisk in sugar and yeast.
3. Mix in water and olive until well-moistened.
4. Knead on a floured surface until smooth (about 3-5 minutes).
5. Cover and rest dough for 15-30 minutes.
6. Sprinkle pizza pan with cornmeal.
7. Place dough on center of pan and press down with your hands to spread up pan edge.
8. Rest dough for 5 minutes.
9. Press down along edge again to spread so that dough hangs over the edges.
10. Line edge with cheese for stuffing.
11. Fold edge over stuffing, pressing down to seal.
12. Top with desired sauce and toppings and bake in a preheated oven at 400°F until lightly browned, about 20-25 minutes.

# Margharita Pizza

*Serves 8 | Prep. time 15 minutes | Cooking time 8 minutes*

### Ingredients
1 (12- to 13-inch) thin crust dough or dough of choice
¼ - ½ cup pizza sauce (p125)
2 cups mozzarella, preferably *di bufala*, freshly shredded
1 Roma tomato, sliced thin
1 tablespoon olive oil
Pinch of sea salt
Freshly ground black pepper
1-2 teaspoons fresh basil leaves

## Directions

1. Preheat oven to 500°F.
2. Spread sauce over dough, about 1 inch from the edge.
3. Sprinkle with cheese. Top with tomato slices.
4. Drizzle with oil and then season with salt and pepper.
5. Bake until golden brown and bubbly (about 8 minutes). Remove from oven.
6. Let rest for the cheese to set about 2-3 minutes. Garnish with basil leaves over top.
7. Slice and serve.

# Aglio E Olio with Cheese Pizza

*Serves 8 | Prep. time 15 minutes | Cooking time 15 minutes*

### Ingredients

cornmeal, for dusting

1 (14- to 16-inch) tossed pizza crust dough, or any of choice

¼ cup garlic, very thinly sliced

1 ½ tablespoons extra-virgin olive oil

½ teaspoon dried oregano

A pinch kosher or sea salt

Freshly ground black pepper, to taste

1 cup mozzarella, freshly shredded

½ cup Fontina, freshly shredded

2 tablespoons parmesan, freshly grated

Fresh chiseled basil, for garnish

### *Directions*

1. Preheat oven to 450°F. Grease pizza pan and dust with cornmeal.
2. Dough may be par-baked just to set (about 5 minutes) or heat for a few minutes in a non-stick pan.
3. Sprinkle garlic over dough and drizzle with olive oil.
4. Sprinkle with dried oregano, salt, pepper, and cheeses.
5. Bake until golden and bubbly, about 15 minutes. Remove from oven.
6. Garnish with chiseled basil and let rest for 2-3 minutes before slicing.

# Neapolitan Pizza

*Serves 6 | Prep. time 15 minutes | Cooking time 3-8 minutes*

### Ingredients
1 thin crust or any dough of choice
1 cup mozzarella di bufala
1-2 cloves garlic, sliced very thinly
2 eggs, beaten
Coarse sea salt and freshly ground black pepper, to taste
Fresh basil leaves
1 tablespoon extra-virgin olive oil

## Directions

1. Preheat oven to hottest temperature (500-550°F for most home ovens), with rack, positioned closest to grill. When well-heated, turn on the grill.
2. Place the crust in a heated skillet or non-stick pan and cook until dough begins to puff up and bottom begins to brown, about 1-3 minutes.
3. Transfer to pan or pizza peel.
4. Tear mozzarella di bufala and scatter over dough.
5. Sprinkle with garlic.
6. Drizzle with beaten eggs over the pizza and season with salt and pepper.
7. Top with basil leaves and drizzle with olive oil.
8. Place under the grill and bake until eggs are just set and crust is browned, about 2-5 minutes.
9. Serve hot.

# Cheese Pizza

*Serves 6 | Prep. time 5 min. | Freeze time 45 min. |*
*Cooking time 10-12 min.*

## Ingredients

1 (12-inch) round of pizza dough (p123)
¼ -⅓ cup pizza sauce (p125) or all-purpose tomato sauce like marinara (p53)
2 cups mozzarella cheese, shredded and then frozen
1 tablespoon fresh basil, chopped finely

## *Directions*

1. Preheat the oven to 450°F 45 minutes to 60 minutes before baking.
2. Keep the grated mozzarella in the freezer for at least 20 minutes.
3. Place the pizza dough on a greased baking pan or pizza stone.
4. Spread the sauce from center of the dough outward, leaving about half an inch of space around the edge.
5. Sprinkle uniformly with shredded mozzarella and basil.
6. Bake until the crust is set and the cheese bubbles, about 10-12 minutes.
7. And Serve!

# Italian Spicy Sausage and Mushrooms Pizza

*Serves 6 | Prep. time 10 min. | Resting time 15 min. Cooking time 25-30 min.*

## Ingredients

1 pound refrigerated ready-made or homemade pizza dough (p123)

Cooking spray

6 ounces spicy Italian sausage (1 large sausage)

1 cup onion, thinly sliced

1 (8-ounce) package mushrooms, sliced

1 cup red or green bell pepper, seeded and diced

1 tablespoon yellow cornmeal, or more, for dusting

½ cup pizza sauce (p125) or all-purpose tomato sauce like marinara (p53)

½ cup shredded mozzarella cheese

¼ cup grated Parmigiano-Reggiano cheese

## Directions

1. Rest the refrigerated dough for 15 minutes.
2. Preheat the oven to 450°F.
3. Remove the sausage from the casing and cook it in a nonstick skillet until it crumbles, about 3 minutes. Break it up with your spatula as it cooks.
4. Add the onions and mushrooms and sauté until tender, about 4 minutes.
5. Add the bell pepper and sauté until fragrant, about 3 minutes.
6. Dust work surface with cornmeal.
7. Pat and stretch the dough gently and place it on the dusted surface.
8. Press it down and spread it with your hands, and then roll it out with a dusted rolling pin to make a 12-inch round.
9. Place the dough on the pizza pan, stretching and shaping it with your hands if needed.
10. Pour the pizza sauce in the center of the dough and spread it to the sides, leaving about half an inch from the edge without sauce.
11. Spread with the sausage and vegetable mixture.
12. Top with mozzarella and then with Parmesan.
13. Bake until the cheese is golden brown and bubbly, about 15-20 minutes.

# MAIN ENTREES

## Chicken Marsala

*Serves 4 | Prep. time 10 minutes | Cooking time 15 minutes*

### *Ingredients*

½ cup all-purpose flour

3 tablespoons olive oil

4 thin chicken cutlets, pounded to a ⅛-inch thickness

Freshly ground black pepper and salt to taste

½ pound button mushrooms, sliced

¾ cup Marsala wine

¼ cup low-sodium chicken stock

## Directions

1. Season the chicken with salt and pepper and coat with the flour. Set aside.
2. Heat the oil in a medium saucepan or skillet over medium heat.
3. Add the chicken and stir-cook to evenly brown for 8–9 minutes.
4. Remove from the pan and set aside.
5. Add the mushrooms and stir-cook for 4–5 minutes.
6. Pour in the wine and cook for a few minutes.
7. Add the stock and bring to a boil over high heat.
8. Mix in the chicken and simmer for a few minutes to thicken the sauce.
9. Serve warm.

# Chicken Palermo

*Serves 4 | Prep. time 15 minutes | Cooking time 20–25 minutes*

**Ingredients**

4 boneless skinless chicken breasts
Salt and pepper
½ cup milk
1½ cups flour
1 egg
1 clove garlic, minced
¼ cup extra virgin olive oil
¼ cup white onions, diced
2 cups white mushrooms, sliced
1 cup chicken broth
1 cup white wine

¼ cup frozen peas
½ cup shredded mozzarella cheese or 4 slices mozzarella cheese
Rice or pasta for serving

## *Directions*

1. Pound the chicken breasts to ¼-inch thick and season with salt and pepper.
2. Combine the egg and milk in a mixing bowl. Add the flour to another bowl.
3. Coat the chicken first in the milk mixture and then in the flour.
4. Refrigerate for at least 1 hour.
5. Pre-heat the oven to $325^0$F.
6. Heat the olive oil in a medium saucepan or skillet over low heat.
7. Add the garlic and cook until fragrant, about 2 minutes.
8. Increase heat to medium-high and add the chicken breasts. Cook 2-3 minutes on each side or until the chicken is cooked through. Remove the pan from the heat and remove the chicken from the pan and place in an oven safe dish. Add mozzarella cheese evenly on each cutlet. Cover loosely with foil and place in the oven to keep warm and let the cheese melt.
9. Add more oil to the pan if necessary and heat to medium-high. Add the onions; stir-cook until softened, about 1-2 minutes. Add the mushrooms and cook until lightly browned, about 2-3 minutes. Increase heat to high and add the broth. Bring to a boil taking care of stirring the bottom of the pan to loosen any bits of flavors stuck to the pan. Add the wine and let sauce thicken. If the sauce becomes too thick, add more wine until desired consistency.
10. Add the peas and cook until heated through, about 1 minute. Remove from heat.
11. To plate, add a chicken cutlet with the melted mozzarella. Top with mushrooms and some of the sauce. Serve with rice or pasta. On the side

# Calabrese Chicken Thighs Sheet Pan Dinner

*Serves 4 | Prep. time 10 minutes | Cooking time 30 minutes*

**Ingredients**
Cooking spray
8 chicken thighs
1 teaspoon salt
1 red onion, sliced

1 red bell pepper, sliced

3 tablespoons extra virgin olive oil

2 teaspoons dried oregano

3 garlic cloves, halved

2–3 sprigs rosemary

3 medium potatoes, peeled and chopped

Ground hot peppers

Juice of 1 lemon

1 dash ground hot peppers

### *Directions*

1. Preheat the oven to 375°F. Grease a baking sheet evenly with cooking spray or line with parchment paper or foil.
2. In a mixing bowl, combine the chicken, salt, onion, red pepper, oil, rosemary, oregano, garlic, and potatoes. Mix well and then mix in the lemon juice and hot pepper. You can add more or less ground hot peppers depending on your taste.
3. Spread the mixture on the baking sheet and bake until the chicken is fully cooked, about 25–35 minutes. Internal temperature should be at least 165°F.
4. Serve warm.

# Tomato Olive Chicken

*Serves 4 | Prep. time 10 minutes | Cooking time 15 minutes*

### Ingredients
1 pint cherry tomatoes, halved

1 teaspoon salt

3 tablespoons olive oil

2 cloves garlic, minced

1 pound chicken tenders, cut into chunks

1 teaspoon dried oregano

¼ cup black or green olives, pitted

## Directions

1. Heat the oil in a medium saucepan or skillet over medium heat.
2. Add the garlic; stir-cook for 1 minute until soft and aromatic.
3. Add the tomatoes and salt; stir-cook for 4–5 minutes.
4. Add the chicken and oregano. Mix well and then add the olives.
5. Cook for 8–10 additional minutes, until the chicken is no longer pink.
6. Serve warm.

# Mushroom Cream Turkey

*Serves 6 | Prep. time 5 minutes | Cooking time 20–25 minutes*

## Ingredients

1 (7-ounce) can peas, drained
2 cloves garlic
4 tablespoons extra-virgin olive oil (divided)
1 small onion, chopped
1 (7-ounce) can mushrooms with juice, finely sliced
1½ pounds turkey breasts, sliced thin
2 tablespoons butter
3½ ounces half and half cream
2 tablespoons tomato sauce
Salt and ground black pepper to taste
All-purpose flour as needed

## Directions

1. In a medium saucepan or skillet over medium heat, heat 1 tablespoon of the olive oil.
2. Add the onion and stir-cook until soft and translucent.
3. Add the peas and 1 tablespoon of hot water; simmer for 5 minutes. Set aside.
4. In another skillet or saucepan, cook the garlic in 1 tablespoon of the olive oil until aromatic.
5. Mix in the mushrooms with juice and simmer for 9–10 minutes. Set aside.
6. In a bowl, coat the turkey slices in the flour.
7. In another skillet, sauté the turkey until evenly brown in the remaining 2 tablespoons of olive oil.
8. Mix in the cream, tomato sauce, cooked peas, and mushrooms.
9. Simmer until the sauce becomes smooth and pink. Add salt and pepper to taste.
10. Serve warm.

# Stewed Beef with Anchovy and Caper Sauce

*Serves 4 | Prep. time 15–20 minutes | Cooking time 90 minutes*

## Ingredients
1 medium onion, thinly sliced
2 pounds rib eye or flank steak
1 clove garlic, minced
2 cups beef broth
1 (2-ounce) can flat anchovy fillets in olive oil, drained
1 tablespoon capers, drained
⅛ teaspoon dried thyme
⅛ teaspoon cracked black pepper
2 tablespoons Parmesan cheese, grated
2–3 slices bacon

## Directions
1. Preheat the oven to 350°F. Grease a baking dish evenly with some cooking spray.
2. Place the onion slices in the baking dish. Arrange the steak over them and rub the garlic into the top side.
3. Top with the anchovy fillets, Parmesan cheese, capers, thyme, pepper, and bacon.
4. Add the broth.
5. Bake uncovered for 1½ hours, or until tender.
6. Slice the steak and serve warm.

# Beef Braciole

*Serves 6 | Prep. time 15–20 minutes | Cooking time 90 minutes*

**Ingredients**
2 pounds boneless top round beef steaks, cut into 12 even pieces
12 slices prosciutto, thin
4 garlic cloves, minced
8 garlic cloves, sliced
½ cup Italian parsley, chopped finely
1 cup grated Parmesan cheese
2 tablespoons Italian seasoned breadcrumbs
Salt and black pepper, to taste
2 tablespoons extra virgin olive oil
2 cups dry red wine
2 cups beef broth
1 (28-ounce) can crushed tomatoes

1 teaspoon dry oregano
1 teaspoon dry basil
½ teaspoon dry thyme
½ teaspoon dry rosemary
2 tablespoons all-purpose flour

For serving
Cooked pasta or polenta
Chopped Italian parsley
Grated Parmesan cheese

### *Directions*

1. On a clean working surface, lay a large piece of plastic wrap. Top with one steak and cover with another layer of plastic wrap. Pound the steak with a mallet or rolling pin to flatten the meat to less than a ¼ inch thick. Repeat for all the steaks.
2. Top each flattened steak with a prosciutto slice.
3. In a mixing bowl, add the 4 minced garlic cloves, parsley, Parmesan cheese, and breadcrumbs. Mix and season to taste with salt and black pepper.
4. Add the breadcrumb mixture evenly on top of each steak. Roll and fold the ends. Close each roll with a toothpick cut in two.
5. Warm the olive oil in deep cast iron pan over medium-high heat. When the oil is hot, brown the rolls on each side. Work in batches so you do not overload the pan. Remove the beef rolls from the pan and let rest on a plate.
6. Increase heat to high and add the wine and bring to a boil, taking care of releasing the brown bits of flavor stuck to the bottom of the pan with a wooden spoon or whisk.
7. Add the 8 sliced garlic cloves, beef broth, tomatoes, oregano, basil, thyme, and rosemary. Let simmer for 10 minutes and decrease the heat to medium-low.
8. Add the beef rolls to the pan, cover with lid or foil, and let simmer on low heat for 1 ½ hours or in the oven pre-heated to 325⁰F. Turn over the beef rolls every 15-20 minutes.
9. When cooked, remove from heat and move beef rolls to a plate. Let rest while thickening the sauce, if needed.
10. Remove about ½ cup of liquid from the pan into a small bowl. Stir-in 2 tablespoons of flour until smooth. Add to the pan, stir well with a whisk or spoon. Increase heat to medium-high and let simmer while stirring until the consistency is just right, about 3 to 6 minutes. Taste the sauce and adjust seasoning with salt and pepper if needed.
11. Add the beef rolls back to the pan and stir. Before serving, take out all toothpicks. Serve over pasta or polenta and sprinkle with parsley and grated Parmesan cheese, if desired.

# Veal Saltimbocca

*Serves 4 | Prep. time 10 minutes | Cooking time 20 minutes*

### Ingredients

4 large veal cutlets
Salt to taste
4 thin slices prosciutto
¾ cup chicken stock
3 tablespoons olive oil
½ cup all-purpose flour
4 tablespoons butter (divided)
8 large sage leaves

## Directions

1. Pound the veal cutlets to flatten to about ¼-inch thick.
2. Lightly season the veal with some salt.
3. Coat the veal with the flour in a mixing bowl
4. Place 2 sage leaves over each cutlet.
5. Top each cutlet with a slice of prosciutto.
6. Heat the oil and 2 tablespoons of the butter in a medium saucepan or skillet over medium heat.
7. Add the coated veal and cook for 8–10 minutes, until cooked well. Work in batches if necessary so you don't overload the pan.
8. Transfer the veal cutlets to a plate.
9. Melt the remaining 2 tablespoons of butter in the saucepan or skillet.
10. Add the chicken stock and bring to a boil. Cook until reduced by half, about 3–4 minutes.
11. Add the cutlets, stir and simmer over medium heat for an additional 2 minutes.
12. Serve warm with pasta if desired.

# Veal Scaloppini Romana

*Serves 6 | Prep. time 10 minutes | Cooking time 45–50 minutes*

### Ingredients

1½ pounds thin veal cutlets, about ¼-inch thick
Salt and pepper
8 tablespoons butter, divided (½ cup – 1 stick)
¾ pound mushrooms, sliced
3 cups tomatoes, peeled and coarsely chopped
1 small onion, finely chopped
1 clove garlic, peeled

⅔ cup dry white wine
¼ teaspoon dried tarragon leaves, crushed
½ tablespoon fresh Italian parsley, minced
Grated Parmesan cheese for garnish (optional)

## *Directions*

1. Season the veal cutlets generously with salt and black pepper.
2. Heat 3 tablespoons of the butter in a skillet or saucepan over medium heat.
3. Add the veal scallops and cook until lightly browned on both sides, about 3–4 minutes per side. Remove from heat and let rest.
4. In another medium saucepan or skillet, heat the remaining 5 tablespoons of the butter over medium heat.
5. Add the mushrooms; stir-cook to evenly brown.
6. Add onion and garlic; cook for 4–5 minutes, until onion is golden.
7. Mix in the tomatoes, wine, tarragon, parsley. Stir gently. Reduce heat to low and simmer, covered, for 30 minutes, stirring periodically. Taste and adjust seasoning with salt and pepper if needed.
8. Add the cooked cutlets; stir. Simmer, covered, for 5 minutes.
9. Serve warm topped with Parmesan cheese, if desired.

# Italian Sausages with Cannellini Beans

*Serves 4 | Prep. time 10 minutes | Cooking time 45–50 minutes*

### Ingredients

1 pound sweet or hot Italian sausages, pricked

2 tablespoons tomato paste

¼ teaspoon salt

⅛ teaspoon pepper

2 tablespoons olive oil

4 cups cooked cannellini beans, drained

¼ cup plus 3 tablespoons water (divided)

## Directions

1. Heat the 3 tablespoons of water in a medium saucepan or skillet over medium heat.
2. Add the sausages and cook until the water evaporates.
3. Continue cooking for 15–20 minutes until the sausage browns on all sides. Remove from pan and set aside.
4. Add the olive oil to the pan and heat it.
5. Stir in the tomato paste, salt, and pepper. Cook for 4–5 minutes.
6. Mix in the cannellini beans, the ¼ cup of water and the sausages.
7. Simmer over medium-low heat for 15 minutes, stirring occasionally.
8. Serve warm.

# Green Olive Pork Tenderloin

*Serves 4 | Prep. time 10 minutes | Cooking time 28 minutes*

### *Ingredients*

1 pork tenderloin, about 1 ½ pounds

Ground black pepper and salt to taste

½ cup all-purpose flour

¼ cup olive oil

3 sprigs rosemary, leaves only plus more for serving

1 cup dry white wine

¾ cup green olives, pitted

## Directions

1. Season pork with salt and pepper and coat with the flour. Set aside for 30 minutes. Slice some of the olives.
2. Preheat the oven to 400$^0$F.
3. Heat the oil and rosemary in a cast iron skillet or oven-safe pan over medium heat.
4. Add the tenderloin; stir-cook to evenly brown on each side, about 2-4 minutes.
5. Add the white wine and olives. Place uncovered in the oven for 20–25 minutes. The internal temperature of the pork should reach at least 145$^0$F, for a touch of pink inside and juicier meat, and up to 160$^0$F, for a well-done meat. Remove from oven and let rest at least 5 minutes before slicing.
6. Serve warm with olives and a drizzle of the cooking juices. Garnish with fresh rosemary.

# Osso Buco in a Tomato Sauce with Creamy Polenta

*Serves 4 | Prep. time 25 minutes | Cooking time 2 hours*

### Ingredients
4 veal shanks, about 8-9 oz. each
½ cup or more all-purpose flour for dusting
2 onions, diced
1-2 carrots, diced, about 1 cup
1 celery stalk, diced
3 cups veal or chicken stock
1 cup dry white wine
1 can Italian-style stewed tomatoes (14 oz.)
1 tablespoon fresh basil, chopped (or 1 teaspoon dry basil)
1 tablespoon fresh sage, chopped (or 1 teaspoon dry sage)
2 tablespoons olive oil
Sea salt and freshly ground black pepper

For Creamy Polenta
1½ cup yellow cornmeal, fine or medium
3 cups milk
3 cups cold water
½ cup butter
1 cup freshly grated Parmesan cheese
1 teaspoon sea salt
Sea salt and freshly ground black pepper

## *Directions*

1. Rinse veal shank under cold water, and pat dry with paper towels.
2. Dust shanks with flour.
3. In a large, deep skillet, warm the olive oil on medium-high heat. When the oil is hot, brown veal shanks on each side until golden brown. Remove veal shanks from skillet and set aside.
4. Add onions, carrots, and celery. Fry for 2-3 minutes until the vegetables are tender and fragrant. Add wine and deglaze by loosening any remaining bits of meat in the skillet.
5. Add veal shanks back to the skillet. Add stock, tomatoes, basil, and sage. Increase the heat to high, and bring to a boil. Season with salt and pepper to taste. Cover with a lid. Reduce heat to medium, and let simmer for 2h00 or until the veal shank are well cooked and tender.
6. In the meantime, prepare the polenta. Add the water, milk, and salt to a large saucepan. Bring to a boil on high heat, whisking continuously to avoid lumps. Reduce heat to medium-low, and let simmer for about 30 minutes. Stir frequently until it becomes thick and velvety. Add Parmesan cheese and butter. Taste and adjust the seasonings with salt and pepper. If the polenta's texture becomes too dense, adjust with some water.
7. To serve, place a generous amount of polenta on plate, and top with a veal shank and its sauce.

# Veal Scaloppini with Lemon Sauce

*Serves 4 | Prep. time 15 minutes | Cooking time 15 minutes*

### Ingredients
1 tablespoon olive oil
3 tablespoons butter
1 pound (4 pieces total) veal scaloppini, flattened
Flour for dredging
Sea salt and freshly ground black pepper
1 glass dry white wine
2 tablespoons fresh lemon juice
2 tablespoons fresh parsley, chopped
½ lemon, sliced

## Preparation method for the scaloppini

1. Pound out the veal with a mallet or rolling pin. It should be very thin.
2. In a large skillet, heat the olive oil and 1 tablespoon of the butter over medium-high heat. When the oil is hot, dredge the veal in flour. Salt and pepper both sides. Dredge only as many as will fit in the skillet.
3. Cook veal about 1 minute on each side, or until cooked through. Remove from skillet and place on an oven-proof platter. Keep them warm, in oven, while remaining veal is cooked.

## Directions for the lemon sauce

1. While veal is in the oven, melt remaining butter in the skillet on medium-high heat. Add the wine and lemon juice. Bring to a boil, and let simmer for 1-2 minutes. Loosen any remaining bits in the pan.
2. To serve, dip each piece of veal in the sauce. and place on warm platter. Garnish with lemon slices and parsley. Drizzle any remaining sauce.

# Herb Grilled Salmon

*Serves 4 | Prep. time 65 minutes | Cooking time 15 minutes*

### Ingredients
4 salmon steaks, about ¾-inch thick
¼ cup of olive oil
¼ cup fresh basil leaves
¼ cup fresh mint leaves
3 tablespoons lemon juice
1 clove garlic, minced
Sea salt and freshly ground pepper

### Directions
1. Combine olive oil, basil, mint, lemon juice. and garlic in small mixing bowl. Beat until well mixed.

2. Salt and pepper salmon steaks. Place them, single layer, in a dish. Pour marinade over. Cover and refrigerate 1 hour, turning after 30 minutes.
3. Preheat grill.
4. Remove salmon from marinade, reserving marinade. Place on hot grill, and cook about 6–7 minutes. Apply reserved marinade, and turn fish. Cook for another 6–7 minutes until salmon flakes easily.
5. Serve with pasta and vegetables. Decorate with basil leaves.

# Rack of Lamb with Rosemary Sauce

*Serves 4 | Prep. time 20 minutes | Marinating time 4 hours |*
*Cooking time 25 minutes*

## Ingredients

2 racks of lamb, about 2 pounds each
Olive oil

Lamb marinade

3 tablespoons Dijon mustard
3 tablespoons fresh rosemary, chopped
1 tablespoon fresh thyme, chopped
3 cloves garlic, minced
½ medium onion, peeled
1 carrot, peeled
Sea salt and freshly ground pepper

Rosemary wine sauce

½ medium onion
3 sprigs fresh rosemary
1 clove garlic, minced finely
½ cup port wine
1 ½ cups chicken broth (low-sodium)
Sea salt and freshly ground pepper

### *Directions*

1. In a food processor, combine all marinade ingredients. Process until smooth. Spread on the lamb. Wrap the racks of lamb in plastic, and let sit in the refrigerator for 3–4 hours. Remove from refrigerator 30 minutes prior to searing.
2. Preheat oven to 375ºF
3. After marinating, remove most of the marinade from lamb, and reserve. Heat a heavy skillet over high heat. Place the rack meaty side down, and sauté until browned. Turn and brown other side.
4. Place lamb in an oven-proof dish. Roast 9 minutes for rare, 12 for medium.
5. Meanwhile, add the onion in the heavy skillet the lamb was browned in over medium-low heat. Add a bit of olive oil if necessary. When onion has caramelized, add rosemary sprigs and garlic. Add the port wine and de-glaze the pan. Add 1 tablespoon of the reserved marinade to the sauce. Add chicken broth and reduce by half. Adjust seasoning with salt and pepper.
6. When lamb is done roasting, slice individual chops and drizzle with rosemary sauce to finish.

# Filet Mignon in Peppercorn Cream Sauce

*Serves 4 | Prep. time 10 minutes | Cooking time 40 minutes*

### Ingredients
4 filet mignon steaks, 1-1½ inch thick
1 tablespoon Dijon mustard
4 tablespoons black peppercorns
½ teaspoon coarse ground salt

For the sauce
3 cups quality red wine such as Cabernet Sauvignon
3 tablespoons butter

2 shallots, minced
1 clove garlic, minced
½ cup brandy
¼ cup heavy cream
¾ cup beef stock
Steamed vegetables for serving
Crunchy onions for topping

### Directions
1. Preheat grill to medium-high.
2. Crush half of the peppercorns by placing the peppercorns in a plastic bag and removing the air. Pound with a heavy rolling pin or mallet.
3. In a saucepan, pour wine, and bring to a boil. Reduce heat to medium, and simmer about 20 minutes, reducing sauce to about ¾ cup. Meanwhile, heat 2 tablespoons of the butter in a skillet along with 1 tablespoon of the peppercorns, the shallot, and the garlic. Sauté for about 2 minutes. Add the brandy, and cook about 5 minutes. Add the cream, stock, remaining round peppercorns, and wine reduction. Simmer over low heat 8-10 minutes while steaks are grilled.
4. Wipe mustard on both sides of the room-temperature steaks. Combine crushed peppercorns and coarse salt on a plate. Press steaks into peppercorn mixture to coat. Place on grill, and cook about 5 minutes on each side for medium-rare.
5. Stir remaining 1 tablespoon butter into wine sauce to thicken. Transfer steaks to serving plates and spoon sauce on the serving plate. Place filet mignon over vegetables. Garnish with crunchy onions.

# Chicken Parmigiana

*Serves 4 | Prep. time 30 minutes | Cooking time 45 minutes*

### Ingredients

4 boneless skinless chicken breast, pounded thin
Salt and pepper
1 large egg, beaten with ½ tablespoon water
½ cup all-purpose flour
1 cup panko bread crumbs
¼ cup vegetable oil
All-Purpose Tomato Sauce, recipe below
1 pound fresh mozzarella, thinly sliced
¼ cup freshly grated Parmesan
Sliced green onion, for garnish
Fettuccini with tomato sauce for serving

All-Purpose Tomato Sauce

2 tablespoons olive oil

1 large onion, finely chopped

4 cloves garlic, smashed to a paste with a pinch of salt

2 (28-ounce) cans plum tomatoes, undrained, pureed in a blender

1 (16-ounce) can crushed tomatoes

1 (2.5-ounce) can tomato paste

1 bay leaf

½ cup Italian parsley

1 small yellow bell pepper, chopped

Salt and freshly ground pepper

## *Directions*

For the sauce

1. In a saucepan, heat the olive oil over medium heat.
2. Cook the onions and garlic until they are soft.
3. Add the pureed tomatoes with their juices, crushed tomatoes, tomato paste, bay leaf, parsley, and bell pepper, and bring it to a boil. Season to taste with salt and pepper.
4. Reduce the heat and cook until slightly thickened, about 30 minutes.
5. Let cool to room temperature and store, refrigerated, in jars.


For the chicken

6. Preheat the oven to 400°F.
7. Season the chicken with salt and pepper
8. Coat with flour and tap lightly to remove any excess.
9. Dip in the egg mixture and all any excess to drip off.
10. Coat evenly with bread crumbs.
11. In a skillet on the stovetop, heat the oil almost to the smoking point.
12. Brown the breasts on both sides, about 30-40 seconds per side.
13. Transfer the chicken to a baking sheet.
14. Top each chicken piece with 1-2 tablespoons of tomato sauce, slices of mozzarella and about 1 tablespoon of Parmesan.
15. Season with salt and pepper.
16. Bake until the chicken is cooked through and the cheese is melted, about 5 to 7 minutes.
17. Garnish with green onion and serve over pasta with tomato sauce if desired.

# Pan-Sheet Italian Sausage Dinner

*Serves 6 | Prep. time 10 minutes | Cooking time 40 minutes*

## Ingredients

6-8 hot Italian pork sausages, cut into 4 pieces
4 bell peppers, seeded and cut into strips
4–5 medium potatoes, peeled and cubed
¼ cup olive oil, plus extra for greasing
Rosemary leaves as needed
1 large onion, sliced
Ground black pepper and salt to taste

### Directions

1. Preheat the oven to 400°F. Grease a baking dish evenly with some cooking spray.
2. Combine the peppers, sausages, potatoes, olive oil, rosemary, and onion in a mixing bowl. Season with salt and pepper.
3. Add the sausage mixture to the baking dish, spreading it evenly. Bake for 35–40 minutes, shaking occasionally to ensure it roasts evenly.
4. Serve warm.

# SIDES

## Stuffed Basil Tomatoes

*Serves 4–6 | Prep. time 15 minutes | Cooking time 20 minutes*

### Ingredients
4–6 large, ripe but firm tomatoes
Ground pepper and salt to taste
6 teaspoons olive oil plus more for brushing
¾ cup mozzarella cheese, shredded
2 teaspoons dried basil
Cooking spray

## Directions

1. Slice the tops from the tomatoes and scoop out the pulp and seeds.
2. Preheat the oven to 375°F. Grease a baking dish evenly with some cooking spray.
3. Add the tomatoes to the baking dish.
4. Season each tomato pocket with salt and pepper. Add 1 teaspoon of olive oil into each tomato.
5. Combine the mozzarella and basil. Stuff the tomatoes with the mozzarella mixture.
6. With a pastry brush, brush the outsides of the tomatoes with some more olive oil.
7. Bake for about 20 minutes, or until the mozzarella has melted. Serve warm.

# Eggplant Parmesan Side

*Serves 6 | Prep. time 10 minutes | Cooking time 15–20 minutes*

## Ingredients

1 large eggplant
1 ½ cups Marinara tomato sauce (p53)
1 egg, beaten lightly
1 cup olive oil
½ teaspoon salt
½ cup grated Parmesan cheese
½ shredded Parmesan cheese

## Directions

1. Preheat the oven to 400°F.
2. Cut the stalk off the eggplant, then peel and cut it into thin slices.
3. Heat the oil in a medium saucepan or skillet over medium heat.
4. Add the eggplant slices; stir-cook until browned on both sides.
5. Sprinkle with salt and drain on paper towels.
6. Arrange half of the eggplant slices in one layer in a casserole dish.
7. Top with half of the tomato sauce and ¼ cup of the grated Parmesan cheese. Repeat the layers.
8. Whisk the egg and the shredded Parmesan cheese in a bowl. Pour over the eggplant. Bake for 12–15 minutes. Serve warm.

# Roasted Italian Vegetables

*Serves 6 | Prep. time 10 minutes | Cooking time 30 minutes*

## Ingredients
2 zucchinis, cut into 1-inch pieces
1½ cups baby potatoes, scrubbed
1 cup baby bella mushrooms, trimmed
1½ cups grape or cherry tomatoes
10 large cloves garlic, smashed
¼ cup extra virgin olive oil or more to taste
1 teaspoon dried thyme
½ tablespoon dried oregano
Salt and ground pepper to taste
Grated Parmesan cheese and pepper flakes for serving

### Directions

1. Preheat the oven to 400°F.
2. Coat the potatoes with some olive oil in a bowl.
3. Place the potatoes over a greased baking sheet. Roast for 10 minutes.
4. In another bowl, combine the olive oil, mushrooms, remaining vegetables, and garlic until coated well.
5. Mix in the dried oregano, thyme, salt, and pepper; combine well.
6. Spread the bowl mixture over a baking sheet. Roast for 18–20 minutes, until tender.
7. Add the mixture to the roasted potatoes and top with the cheese and pepper flakes. Serve warm.

# Aromatic Oregano Peppers

*Serves 8 | Prep. time 8–10 minutes | Cooking time 15 minutes*

**Ingredients**

2 tablespoons olive oil

3 garlic clove, chopped

4 large red bell peppers

2 tablespoons butter

¼ teaspoon oregano

⅛ teaspoon black pepper

Salt to taste

### Directions

1. Remove the stems, pith, and seeds from the peppers. Cut into strips lengthwise.
2. Heat the oil in a medium saucepan or skillet over medium heat.
3. Add the butter and melt it. Add the pepper strips and garlic; stir-cook to soften and turn light brown.
4. Sprinkle with the oregano and black pepper.
5. Cover the pan and cook over low heat for 15 minutes or just until limp and tender.
6. Season with salt and serve warm.

# Sicilian Stuffed Artichokes

*Serves 4 | Prep. time 15 minutes | Cooking time 45 minutes*

## Ingredients

4 artichokes
1 tablespoon fresh parsley, chopped
3 tablespoons pecorino romano or Parmesan cheese, grated
1 ½ cups breadcrumbs
½ onion, diced
2 garlic cloves, minced
½ teaspoon salt
½ teaspoon pepper
2 tablespoons water
2 tablespoons olive oil
¼ cup extra-virgin olive oil

### Directions

1. Preheat the oven to 325°F.
2. Cut the stalks and tips off the artichokes and remove the tough outer leaves. Spread the remaining leaves open.
3. In a mixing bowl, mix the onion, garlic, parsley, cheese, breadcrumbs, salt, and pepper.
4. Add the ¼ cup of extra-virgin olive oil and 2 tablespoons of water; mix well.
5. Fill each artichoke leaf with a bit of the mixture. Fill the center of each artichoke with the same mixture.
6. Pour a little water in the bottom of a baking dish and arrange the artichokes. Sprinkle with the 2 tablespoons of olive oil.
7. Bake for 45 minutes or until the bottoms of the artichokes turn soft.
8. Serve warm.

# DESERTS

## Ravioli Dolci

*Yields 25–30 raviolis | Prep. time 20–25 minutes | Cooking time 10–15 minutes*

### Ingredients
1½ tablespoons butter
1¾ cups flour
1½ tablespoons vegetable shortening
½ pound ricotta cheese
2 ounce semi-sweet chocolate, melted
2 egg yolks
1 egg white
2 tablespoons granulated sugar

½ teaspoon vanilla extract
Vegetable oil and water as needed
Confectioners' sugar as needed

### *Directions*

1. In a mixing bowl, combine the flour, butter, shortening, and water to form a stiff dough. Add more water if needed.
2. Roll the dough over a floured surface to make a thin layer. Cut into 2-inch squares.
3. In another mixing bowl, combine the ricotta, chocolate, egg white, egg yolks, sugar, and vanilla.
4. Add a teaspoonful of filling to the center of each prepared square. Place another square on top.
5. Seal the edges tight with a fork.
6. Heat the oil in a frying pan over medium heat.
7. Add the ravioli and fry until golden brown.
8. Drain on paper towels. Sprinkle with confectioners' sugar.

# Citrus Ciambella

*Serves 10 | Prep. time 10 minutes | Cooking time 35 minutes*

### Ingredients

1½ cups granulated sugar

1 tablespoon lemon zest

½ cup lemon juice

5 large eggs

½ cup light-tasting olive oil

2 cups all-purpose flour

2 teaspoons baking powder

½ teaspoon salt

Confectioners' sugar (optional)

Nonstick cooking spray

## Directions

1. Preheat the oven to 350°F. Spray a Bundt pan with cooking spray.
2. In a mixing bowl, mix the sugar, eggs, and zest. Whisk well.
3. Mix in the lemon juice and oil.
4. Add the flour, baking powder and salt. Combine well.
5. Pour the batter into the prepared pan and bake for 35–40 minutes until a toothpick inserted comes out clean.
6. Dust with confectioners' sugar (if using).

# Nutty Cantucci

*Yields 24 cookies| Prep. time 15 minutes | Cooking time 40 minutes*

## Ingredients

2 cups all-purpose flour

¼ teaspoon salt

2 large eggs

1 large egg yolk, lightly beaten

1 cup sugar

1 teaspoon baking powder

Zest of 1 large orange

1 cup hazelnuts or almonds, roughly chopped

Cooking spray

### *Directions*

1. Preheat the oven to 350°F / 176°C. Grease a baking sheet evenly with cooking spray.
2. Mix the flour, sugar, baking powder and salt in a mixing bowl.
3. Make a well in the middle and add the eggs and zest.
4. Combine to form a dough.
5. Add the nuts and continue mixing.
6. Divide the dough in half and prepare two logs.
7. Arrange the logs on the baking sheet several inches apart.
8. Bake for 22–25 minutes.
9. Cool down for 10 minutes and cut the logs diagonally into slices.
10. Arrange them back on the baking sheet, cut-side down.
11. Set oven temperature to 325°F / 162°C.
12. Bake for 10–15 more minutes, turning halfway.
13. Serve warm.

# Classic Tiramisu

*Serves 6 | Preparation: 3h30 minutes or more*

### Ingredients

1½ pounds mascarpone
6 eggs
⅔ cup sugar
2 teaspoons of vanilla
1 cup Espresso – very strong
Amaretto liquor (optional)
18 Ladyfingers cookies
Cocoa powder
Mint leaves for decoration

## Directions

1. Beat eggs, sugar, and vanilla about 8-10 minutes, until it's very smooth and the cream has become fluffy and almost white. Incorporate the mascarpone cheese, and mix for an additional 4 to 6 minutes.
2. Prepare the espresso so it is very strong. Pour the coffee into a shallow bowl, and if desired, add some amaretto to taste. Break the ladyfinger cookies in two before soaking. Soak the cookies one piece at a time very quickly, literally in and out of the coffee. Let rest on a plate.
3. To assemble the tiramisu, deposit 1 tablespoon of the mascarpone cream at the bottom of serving glass, just so it barely covers the bottom. Place 2 or 3 pieces of the soaked cookie, and cover with the mascarpone cream. Lightly sprinkle with cocoa powder. Repeat another layer of cookies and cream and cocoa powder until the glass is almost filled. Finish with the cocoa powder.
4. Refrigerate at least 3 hours before you are ready to serve.
5. Decorate with fresh mint leaves.

# Traditional Panna Cotta with Berries

*Serving: 4 | Preparation: 6h20 minutes or more*

## Ingredients

2 cups heavy cream

2½ tablespoons granulated sugar

3 tablespoons milk

1 gelatin leave*

1 vanilla bean pod – scraped seeds

<u>For the topping</u>
1 ½ cup fresh berries of your choice
¼ cup sugar
¼ cup water
Mint leaves

## *Directions*

1. Place gelatin leaf in a saucepan with cold water. Place saucepan over medium-high heat and just before it starts to boil, remove the saucepan from the heat and squeeze gelatin. Add milk to a small bowl. Add gelatin to the milk. Stir gelatin with a spoon until dissolved.
2. Combine fresh cream with the sugar and vanilla seeds in a medium saucepan. Heat over medium-high heat and bring to boil, stirring frequently.
3. When it boils remove from the heat and add milk-gelatin mixture. Mix well and pour into 4 ramekins. Place in refrigerator, overnight or at least for 6 hours.
4. Prepare the topping; Combine sugar and water in a small saucepan and heat over medium-high. Bring to simmer and continue simmering for 5 minutes; add berries and stir well. Let it simmer for 2-3 minutes and set aside to cool.
5. To remove from the molds, place the ramekins in a bowl of boiling water for 1-2 minutes. With a knife, delicately unmold the sides, reverse and place on a plate. Drizzle with prepared berries topping. Decorate with mint leaves.

*Note: you can find gelatin leaves in fine Italian grocery stores.*

*If you cannot find any, you can use 1 teaspoon of unflavored gelatin powder (half a packet). The method to prepare the gelatin to add to the cream mixture is to sprinkle the gelatin with 1½ tablespoon of cold water in a small bowl. Stir with a spoon and let it rest for 10 minutes until the gelatin has dissolved. Continue the recipe as described.*

# Raspberry Zabaglione

*Serves 4 | Prep. Time 10 minutes | Cooking time 25-30 minutes*

## Ingredients

1 cup fresh raspberries, plus some more for garnish
⅓ cup sugar plus 1 tablespoon
1 cup Vin Santo or Marsala
4 large egg yolks
4 Ladyfinger cookies

## *Directions*

1. Place raspberries in a medium-sized saucepan. Sprinkle with sugar, just to taste. Cook on medium-high heat for 3-4 minutes until raspberries are soft, and the mixture is syrupy. Transfer to 4 dessert glasses. Set aside.
2. Whisk sugar and egg yolks in a heat-proof bowl until pale and thick. You can use an electric whisk for this step.
3. Place the bowl over a pan of simmering water, and whisk on low speed for 15 minutes. Drizzle the wine into it, and continue cooking until the mixture almost triples and has soft peaks.
4. Spoon on top of raspberries. Add fresh raspberries and a ladyfinger cookie on top. Serve while still warm.

# Sicilian Cake

*Serves 8 | Prep. Time 90 minutes | Cooking time 10 minutes*

**Ingredients**

4 oz. marzipan

1 ½ cups ricotta cheese

6 oz. powdered sugar

3 oz. candied fruits

3 oz. dark chocolate

4 oz. sponge cake

3 oz. chocolate chips

1 teaspoon vanilla extract

3 tablespoons rum

For icing

1 cup sugar

1 egg white

*To garnish:*
Some candied fruits and other cake decorations

### Directions
1. Roll out the marzipan onto parchment paper to 1/8-inch thin.
2. Dust an 8-inch cake pan with powdered sugar, and line with the marzipan. Slightly press so it adheres perfectly. Trim the edges with a sharp knife. Melt the chocolate over a double boiler, and brush the marzipan with chocolate.
3. Cut cake sponge into thin strips around ½-inch wide. Line the cake pan with them, bottom and sides. Leave some for the top. Brush sponge cake with half of the rum.
4. In a medium-sized bowl, combine ricotta cheese, chocolate chips, remaining sugar, vanilla extract, and chopped candied fruits. Mix well to combine. Transfer to the cake pan, and layer on top of sponge cake. Top with remaining sponge cake stripes, and brush with rum.
5. Place the cake in the freezer for 15 minutes before unmolding on a service plate.
6. For the glaze: Whisk egg white with sugar, until thick and heavy. Pour over the prepared cake, and set aside for 1 hour.
7. Garnish with some candied fruits and any other cake decorations.

# Crème Caramel

*Serving: 4 | Prep. Time 10 minutes | Cooking time 75 minutes*

## Ingredients

¼ cup sugar
½ pint milk
2 eggs
¼ cup sugar – for the caramel
1 vanilla pod, seeds scraped
½ teaspoon lemon juice
Small pinch of salt

## Directions

1. Place sugar in a saucepan with lemon juice and salt; heat over medium-low heat. Stir until sugar dissolves and caramel forms. Pour caramel in an 8-inch round ramekin mold or in 4 individual ramekins.
2. Gently heat milk in another saucepan and add vanilla seeds.
3. Beat 1 egg and just 1 egg yolk with remaining sugar, until well whisked. Gradually add milk in the egg mixture and whisk constantly, until all milk is incorporated.
4. Preheat oven to 275ºF.
5. Pour the milk in the mold on top of the caramel. Place the mold in a larger dish filled with about 2-inch of water. Bake for 1 hour. Allow cooling before you remove from the mold.

# Homemade Cannoli

*Serves 12 | Prep. time 20 min. | Chill time 2 hours |
Cooking time 10-15 minutes*

### Ingredients
Egg white, for sealing
Oil for frying, 3 inches deep

Cannoli shell
2 ⅓ cups flour
1 ½ tablespoons sugar
2 tablespoons butter
1 egg
⅛ teaspoon salt
¾ cup Marsala dry wine

<u>Cream Filling</u>
2 cups ricotta cheese
2 cups confectioner's sugar, sifted
2 tablespoons rum
¼ teaspoon vanilla extract
3 ounces bitter chocolate, broken into tiny chips

***Directions***

<u>To make the shells</u>
1. In a large bowl, mix the shell ingredients together to make a smooth, slightly sticky dough.
2. Wrap the dough in plastic wrap and refrigerate for 2 hours to overnight.
3. Cut the dough into two pieces. Keep the remaining dough covered and cold while you work.
4. Lightly flour a work surface and roll out the dough to about ⅛ inch thick.
5. Cut out circles, 3 to 5 inches in diameter.
6. Roll each cutout circle into an oval.
7. Oil the outside of the cannoli tubes. You can also use cannelloni pasta as tubes.
8. Roll the ovals around each tube and dab a little egg white on the dough where the edges overlap. Press well to seal. Let them sit for the egg white to set.
9. In a heavy saucepan or electric deep-fryer, heat the oil to 375°F, or until a small piece of the dough sizzles and browns in 1 minute.
10. Fry the shells until golden, turning halfway through (about 2 minutes).
11. Lift with a wire skimmer or large slotted spoon. Using tongs, grasp the cannoli vertically over the fryer to let the oil flow back into the pan.
12. Drain on paper towels. Repeat with the remaining tubes.
13. While still hot, grasp the tubes with a potholder and, using a pair of tongs, pull the cannoli shells off.
14. Let cool completely on the paper towels.

<u>For the filling</u>
15. In a large bowl, cream the ricotta with a wire whisk.
16. Add the rest of the ingredients and mix thoroughly.
17. Fill a pastry tube, and pipe the filling into the shells.
18. Dust with confectioner's sugar, and serve.

# Wine Zabaglione

*Serves 6 | Prep. time 5 minutes | Cooking time 15 minutes*

## Ingredients

1 cup granulated sugar
¼ cup Marsala wine
6 large egg yolks
Berries of your choice to serve

## Directions

1. Combine the egg yolks and sugar in a mixing bowl.
2. Place the bowl in a double boiler.
3. Over low heat, add the eggs and sugar. Whisk the mixture constantly to ensure that the eggs don't scramble.
4. Mix in the wine until the cream thickens, about 10–15 minutes.
5. Serve warm with some fresh berries on top or refrigerate for a few hours and serve chilled.

# RECIPE INDEX

More cookbooks from Sarah Spencer:

# APPENDIX

# Cooking Conversion Charts

## 1. Measuring Equivalent Chart

| Type | Imperial | Imperial | Metric |
|------|----------|----------|--------|
| Weight | 1 dry ounce | | 28 g |
| | 1 pound | 16 dry ounces | 0.45 kg |
| Volume | 1 teaspoon | | 5 ml |
| | 1 dessert spoon | 2 teaspoons | 10 ml |
| | 1 tablespoon | 3 teaspoons | 15 ml |
| | 1 Australian tablespoon | 4 teaspoons | 20 ml |
| | 1 fluid ounce | 2 tablespoons | 30 ml |
| | 1 cup | 16 tablespoons | 240 ml |
| | 1 cup | 8 fluid ounces | 240 ml |
| | 1 pint | 2 cups | 470 ml |
| | 1 quart | 2 pints | 0.95 l |
| | 1 gallon | 4 quarts | 3.8 l |
| Length | 1 inch | | 2.54 cm |

\*  Numbers are rounded to the closest equivalent

## 2. Oven Temperature Equivalent Chart

| Fahrenheit (°F) | Celsius (°C) | Gas Mark |
| --- | --- | --- |
| 220 | 100 | |
| 225 | 110 | 1/4 |
| 250 | 120 | 1/2 |
| 275 | 140 | 1 |
| 300 | 150 | 2 |
| 325 | 160 | 3 |
| 350 | 180 | 4 |
| 375 | 190 | 5 |
| 400 | 200 | 6 |
| 425 | 220 | 7 |
| 450 | 230 | 8 |
| 475 | 250 | 9 |
| 500 | 260 | |

\*   Celsius (°C) = T (°F)-32] * 5/9

\*\*  Fahrenheit (°F) = T (°C) * 9/5 + 32

\*\*\* Numbers are rounded to the closest equivalent

# Image Credits

*Marinara Pizza*

*Stuffed Crust Pizza*

*Neapolitan Pizza*

Made in the USA
Coppell, TX
05 January 2023